Tobacco

PEOPLE
PROFITS
&
PUBLIC HEALTH

IDEAS in CONFLICT

Gary E. McCuen

GEM
GARY McCUEN
publications inc.

411 Mallalieu Drive
Hudson, Wisconsin 54016
Phone (715) 386-7113

Illustration and Photo Credits

Center for Disease Control 25, 53, 83, 88; Federal Trade Commission 47; Steve Kelly 137; Gary Markstein 109; Wayne Stayskal 117; Richard Wright 74, 131.

© 1997 by Gary E. McCuen Publications, Inc.
411 Mallalieu Drive, Hudson, Wisconsin 54016

(715) 386-7113

International Standard Book Number
0-86596-142-5
Printed in the United States of America

CONTENTS

IDEAS IN CONFLICT

Chapter 1   TOBACCO, HEALTH AND SAFETY

Chapter 2   HOOKED ON SMOKING

REASONING SKILL DEVELOPMENT

These activities may be used as individualized study guides for students in libraries and resource centers or as discussion catalysts in small group and classroom discussions.

IDEAS
in CONFLICT

This series features ideas in conflict on political, social, and moral issues. It presents counterpoints, debates, opinions, commentary, and analysis for use in libraries and classrooms. Each title in the series uses one or more of the following basic elements:

Introductions that present an issue overview giving historic background and/or a description of the controversy.

Counterpoints and debates carefully chosen from publications, books, and position papers on the political right and left to help librarians and teachers respond to requests that treatment of public issues be fair and balanced.

Symposiums and forums that go beyond debates that can polarize and oversimplify. These present commentary from across the political spectrum that reflect how complex issues attract many shades of opinion.

A *global* emphasis with foreign perspectives and surveys on various moral questions and political issues that will help readers to place subject matter in a less culture-bound and ethnocentric frame of reference. In an ever-shrinking and interdependent world, understanding and cooperation are essential. Many issues are global in nature and can be effectively dealt with only by common efforts and international understanding.

Reasoning skill study guides and discussion activities provide ready-made tools for helping with critical reading and evaluation of content. The guides and activities deal with one or more of the following:

RECOGNIZING AUTHOR'S POINT OF VIEW

INTERPRETING EDITORIAL CARTOONS

VALUES IN CONFLICT

WHAT IS EDITORIAL BIAS?

WHAT IS SEX BIAS?

WHAT IS POLITICAL BIAS?

WHAT IS ETHNOCENTRIC BIAS?

WHAT IS RACE BIAS?

WHAT IS RELIGIOUS BIAS?

*From across **the political spectrum** varied sources are presented for research projects and classroom discussions. Diverse opinions in the series come from magazines, newspapers, syndicated columnists, books, political speeches, foreign nations, and position papers by corporations and nonprofit institutions.*

About the Editor

Gary E. McCuen is an editor and publisher of anthologies for libraries and discussion materials for schools and colleges. His publications have specialized in social, moral and political conflict. They include books, pamphlets, cassettes, tabloids, filmstrips and simulation games, most of them created from his many years of experience in teaching and educational publishing.

CHAPTER 1

TOBACCO, HEALTH, AND SAFETY

THE GLOBAL PUBLIC HEALTH EMERGENCY

World Health Organization

The World Health Organization (WHO), based in Geneva, was formed in April 1948 after the United Nations ratified the Constitution of the World Health Organization. WHO maintains the objective of promoting the physical, mental and social health of all peoples. Currently, Dr. Hiroshi Nakajima serves as Director General of WHO.

■ POINTS TO CONSIDER

1. Discuss the trends in tobacco consumption around the world.

2. How has smoking affected men and women respectively? How are trends in smoking among men and women changing, and what effects will this have?

3. Is either the consumption or production of tobacco concentrated in any part of the world, according to WHO?

4. Describe various tobacco control measures accepted by nations. What are some of the effects of these control measures?

Excerpted from the World Health Organization Fact Sheet N° 118, "The Tobacco Epidemic: A Global Public Health Emergency," May 1996. Reprinted by permission WHO, 20, Avenue Appia, 1211 GENEVA 27, Switzerland.

Tobacco is estimated to have caused around three million deaths a year in the early 1990s, and the death toll is steadily increasing.

TOBACCO USE

By the end of the 20th century, manufactured cigarettes have come to be the predominant form by which tobacco is consumed around the world. However there are many other methods by which tobacco is consumed, and in some regions, these other forms predominate. In India, for example, eight times more *bidis* (tobacco wrapped in a temburni leaf) than manufactured cigarettes are consumed annually.

Global consumption of cigarettes per adult has remained steady from the early 1970s to the early 1990s; however, as the global population has continued to increase, the absolute number of cigarettes consumed has continued to increase.

According to WHO estimates, there are around 1.1 thousand million smokers in the world, about one-third of the global population aged 15 years and over. In recent years, tobacco use has been declining in many countries of North America and Western Europe, but increasing in many developing countries, particularly in Asia.

GROWTH IN DEVELOPING NATIONS

In China, the growth in estimated per capita consumption of cigarettes has been particularly rapid, increasing by 260% from the early 1970s to the early 1990s, with consumption estimated at around 1900 cigarettes per adult per year. In China there are about 300 million smokers, about the same number as in all developed countries combined.

China, the world's most populous country is also the world's leading consumer of cigarettes. The world's second most populous country, India, ranks only 14th for manufactured cigarettes, however when *bidis* are taken into account, India ranks second globally for total cigarette consumption.

Substantially fewer cigarettes are smoked per day per smoker in developing countries than in developed countries. In the early 1990s, average adult per capita consumption in developed countries was 2590 v. 1410 in developing countries. However, the gap in per adult cigarette consumption is narrowing. Unless effective tobacco control measures take place, daily cigarette consumption in developing countries is expected to increase as economic development results in increased real disposable income. If current trends continue, per adult consumption in developing countries will exceed that of developed countries shortly after the turn of the century.

WHO is concerned about the decreasing age of smoking initiation. Data revealed that in many countries, the median age of smoking initiation was under the age of 15. This is of particular concern, since starting to smoke at younger ages increases the risk of death from a smoking-related cause. Among those who continue to smoke throughout their lives, about half can be expected to die from a smoking-related cause, with half of those deaths occurring in middle age. In countries such as France and Spain where more than 40% of young people aged 18-24 smoke (and most beginning at an early age) a very heavy future death toll from tobacco use can be expected.

SMOKING PREVALENCE

The WHO report provides first-time estimates of worldwide smoking prevalence, based on surveys conducted in 87 countries, accounting for 85% of the world's population.

- Globally, approximately 47% of men and 12% of women smoke.

- In developing countries, available data suggest that 48% of men smoke, as do 7% of women, while in developed countries, 42% of men and 24% of women smoke.

- Of the 87 countries for which data was available, male smoking prevalence is 50% or more in 22 countries, while female smoking prevalence is 25% or more in 26 countries.

- In countries with established market economies, male smoking prevalence averages around 37%, compared to 60% in the countries of Central and Eastern Europe.

- Smoking among women is most prevalent in the countries of Central and Eastern Europe (28%), countries with established market economies (23%) and Latin American and Caribbean countries (21%). In all other regions, fewer than 10% of women smoke.

- About one-third of regular smokers in developed countries are women, compared with only about one in eight in the developing world.

- Three countries, the Russian Federation, Poland and Fiji, rank in the top twenty for both male and female smoking prevalence.

HEALTH EFFECTS

Tobacco is estimated to have caused around three million deaths a year in the early 1990s, and the death toll is steadily increasing. Unless current trends are reversed, that figure is expected to rise to 10 million deaths per year by the 2020s or the early 2030s (by the time the young smokers of today reach middle and older ages), with 70% of those deaths occurring in developing countries. The chief uncertainty is not whether these deaths will occur, but exactly when.

The increase in the epidemic of smoking-caused mortality in developed countries is slowing somewhat among men, but continues to increase rapidly among women, even if the epidemic of smoking-related death is not as advanced as among men. In the mid 1990s, about 25% of all male deaths in developing countries were due to smoking, and among middle aged men (aged 35-69), more than one-third of all deaths were caused by smoking. For middle-aged women in developed countries, the percentage of all deaths caused by smoking increased more than six-fold, from 2% in 1955 to 13% in 1995, and continues to increase rapidly.

Of all the diseases causally associated with smoking, lung cancer is the most well known, largely because in most populations, almost all lung cancer deaths are due to smoking. However, smoking actually causes more deaths from diseases other than lung cancer. In 1995, there were 514,000 smoking-caused lung cancer deaths in developed countries, compared to 625,000 smoking-attributable deaths from heart and other vascular diseases in the same year.

Smokeless tobacco also poses serious health risks. The annual mortality from tobacco chewing in South Asia alone may well be of the order of 50,000 deaths a year.

TOBACCO PRODUCTION AND TRADE

Most of the global tobacco manufacturing industry is controlled by a small number of state monopolies and multinational corporations. The largest of these is the state monopoly in China, which in 1993 represented 31% of the global market. In 1993, the seven largest multinational tobacco corporations accounted for nearly 40% of global cigarette sales.

China is the world's dominant producer of unmanufactured tobacco, producing as much as the next seven largest producers combined. While tobacco is grown in over 100 countries, the 25 leading producers account for over 90% of global tobacco production. Worldwide, just four countries, China, the U.S., Japan and Germany account for over half of global production.

The United States is a major cigarette production center and the world's leading exporter of manufactured cigarettes. For a number of years, the United States was the world's leading exporter of unmanufactured tobacco. However, by 1994, it had been surpassed by Brazil and Zimbabwe, the two leading sources of internationally traded unmanufactured tobacco as of the mid 1990s.

13

Just five countries, Brazil, Zimbabwe, the United States, Turkey and Italy account for over half of all global exports of unmanufactured tobacco. Tobacco is also economically important in Brazil, the world's largest tobacco leaf exporter.

TOBACCO CONTROL MEASURES

From 1970 to 1995, the World Health Assembly adopted 14 resolutions, all without dissent, in favor of tobacco control measures. Several of these resolutions called for comprehensive tobacco control programs and policies.

In the early 1990s, about 25 countries had laws that prohibited the sale of cigarettes to minors, with the age of prohibition ranging from 16 to 21 years of age. In some cases, other related measures have been enacted, including bans or restrictions on cigarette sales from vending machines, prohibitions on sales of tobacco products and smoking in schools, prohibiting the sale of single cigarettes and banning the offering of free samples of cigarettes.

There are active programs to train pharmacists in smoking cessation counselling in Belgium, Denmark and the United Kingdom, with more European countries expected to follow suit. Telephone counselling services (quit lines) to assist people who wish to quit smoking are offered in a number of Member States. In Australia and South Africa, quit line telephone numbers are included along with required health information printed on every package of cigarettes.

In the early 1990s, about 80 countries required health warnings to appear on packages of tobacco products. However, in most of these countries, the warnings are small and provide little information about the many serious health consequences of tobacco use. By the mid 1990s, however, a number of countries had adopted more stringent warning systems, involving direct statements of health hazards, multiple messages, as well as large and prominent display. Such warnings are presently required in a number of countries including Australia, Canada, Iceland, Norway, Singapore, South Africa and Thailand.

As of 1990, 27 countries reportedly had total or near-total bans on advertising. Since then, however, the number has declined to 18. While Australia and Kuwait recently implemented bans on tobacco advertising, tobacco advertising bans that had been in place became inoperative in Canada and the newly independent

SMOKING IN AMERICA

Although the prevalence of smoking declined from 42.4% of the adult population (age 18 and over) in 1965 to 25.7% in 1991, the number of adult smokers remained relatively unchanged because of the increase in the size of the U.S. population. There were an estimated 50.1 million cigarette smokers in the United States in 1965, 53.5 million in 1983, and 46.3 million in 1991. The number of never smokers also increased from 52.0 million in 1965 to 90.6 million in 1991. Many smokers quit during this period, and by 1991 there were almost as many former smokers (43.5 million) as current smokers in the United States. Nevertheless, nicotine dependency proves to be a significant obstacle to quitting. Approximately 70% of current smokers say they want to quit smoking, but only about half attempt to quit each year. Of those that attempt to quit smoking, only one in 13 succeeds.

Smoking is the leading preventable cause of death in the United States. In 1990, almost 419,000 deaths – about 20% of all deaths reported that year – were attributable, at least in part, to smoking. Epidemiologists in Britain and the United States now estimate that half of all lifetime smokers will die from a smoking-related illness, approximately one-quarter in old age and one-quarter in middle age (35-69). Those that die from a smoking-related illness in middle age lose an average of 20-25 years of non-smoker life expectancy.

Tobacco is a major risk factor for heart disease, stroke, chronic bronchitis and emphysema, and cancer of the lung, throat, mouth, esophagus, bladder and pancreas. Cigarette smoking is responsible for approximately 20% of all heart disease deaths and 30% of all cancer deaths, including more than 80% of lung cancer deaths. Between 20 and 30% of the incidence of low birth weight babies, and about 14% of all infant deaths are attributable to smoking during pregnancy. Compared to nonsmokers, cigarette smokers miss an additional 6.5 work days per year and make about six additional visits to health care facilities per year.

"Smoking – A Fact Sheet," Congressional Research Service Report, July 25, 1996.

states of Central and Eastern Europe. However, Canada and many Central and East European countries are considering draft legislation to re-establish bans on tobacco advertising.

A number of countries have successfully used a portion of tobacco taxation revenue to offset the cost of operating their comprehensive tobacco control programs. In several Australian states, tobacco taxes are used to finance Health Promotion Foundations. A similar foundation exists in New Zealand funded from general revenue. In Finland, 0.45% of tobacco taxation revenue is allocated for tobacco control activities. In other countries, such as Nepal, Portugal, Romania and Switzerland, a portion of tobacco tax revenue is used to finance specific health or social programs.

Several WHO Member States have long-standing comprehensive tobacco control policies, built up gradually since the 1970s. As of the mid 1990s, Finland, Iceland, Norway, Portugal and Singapore fit into this category. Other countries, such as Australia, France, New Zealand, Sweden and Thailand have more recently implemented truly comprehensive tobacco control programs which encompass most or all of the nine elements called for by the 1986 World Health Assembly resolution.

READING

2

SMOKELESS TOBACCO INDUSTRY MANIPULATES NICOTINE LEVELS

Gregory N. Connolly

Gregory N. Connolly, D.M.D, M.P.H. is a dentist and public health official with the Massachusetts Department of Public Health. He serves as Director of the Tobacco Control Program. The following remarks were prepared on behalf of the Coalition on Smoking OR Health.

■ **POINTS TO CONSIDER**

1. Discuss the trends in smokeless tobacco use since 1970. Why do the trends alarm the author?

2. Why are pH levels important in the discussion of smokeless tobacco, according to the author?

3. Summarize the concept of "graduation strategy" in tobacco manufacture. What evidence does the author give for this strategy, and what are the motives behind it?

4. Why is Connolly critical of the marketing and advertising strategy of the smokeless tobacco industry? What are the implications for children?

Excerpted from the testimony of Gregory N. Connolly, D.M.D., M.P.H. before the Subcommittee on Health and Environment of the House of Representatives Committee on Energy and Commerce, Nov. 29, 1994.

Oral snuff manufacturers intentionally control the
nicotine levels delivered to their consumers...

Oral snuff is a finely cut processed tobacco which the user places between the cheek and gums. In 1986 the Surgeon General concluded that use of these products causes oral cancer, gum disease and nicotine addiction. More recent research suggests that snuff increases risk of cardiovascular disease including heart attack.

INCREASED USE IN THE U.S.

In recent years use of oral snuff has risen dramatically among young males. From 1970 to 1991, the prevalence of use of snuff by men 18+ rose from 1.4% to 3.1% and among males 18-19 from .3% in 1970 to 7.6%, making that age group the heaviest users of the product. The 1990 Youth Risk Behavior Survey found that 24 percent of all white male high school students used smokeless tobacco at least once during the past month. A 1989 National Collegiate Athletic Association (NCAA) survey of college athletes found a 40 percent increase (from 20% to 28%) in the use of smokeless tobacco from 1985 to 1989. Among NCAA baseball players an alarming 57 percent use. This increase is no accident but a direct result of a sophisticated marketing campaign that advertised and promoted the use of low nicotine oral snuff starter products as part of a graduation strategy that intended new users to graduate up to higher nicotine brands as dependence progressed. These brands are highly addictive and high in cancer causing agents called nitrosamines.

MANIPULATION OF NICOTINE LEVELS

Oral snuff manufacturers intentionally control the nicotine levels delivered to their consumers by controlling the amount of total nicotine in their brands and the level of free nicotine that is available for uptake into the body.

Free nicotine refers to unprotonated nicotine which is rapidly absorbed across the membranes of the mouth into the body. Free nicotine is formed as the pH of the tobacco increases. At a nearly neutral pH of 6.0 no nicotine is unprotonated; at a pH of 8.0 about 70% is.

Total nicotine is controlled through selection and blending of the tobacco leaf. Free nicotine levels are controlled through fer-

18

mentation and/or the addition of alkaline buffering agents such as sodium carbonate and ammonium carbonate. These two additives appear on the additive list that the industry trade association, the Smokeless Tobacco Council, supplied to the Subcommittee. Mr. Taddeo, (president of U.S. Tobacco), denied controlling nicotine in UST products at the April 1994 hearing of the Subcommittee. However, the Swedish Tobacco Company, which also manufactures oral snuff, readily admits controlling nicotine bioavailability.

STARTER BRANDS AND THE "GRADUATION" STRATEGY

If a new user starts with the standard high nicotine brands such as Skoal Fine Cut or Copenhagen, a toxic response such as dizziness or nausea may occur and a new user is more likely to quit before tolerance to the toxic effects of nicotine develops. To respond to this problem and expand its user base U.S. Tobacco (UST) developed low nicotine starter brands: first Happy Days, in the late 1960's and then Skoal Bandits in 1983 and Skoal Long Cut in 1984. These brands were much more heavily advertised than Skoal Fine Cut or Copenhagen and the only ones free sampled. The company also developed a graduation strategy that called for new users to "graduate" up to higher brands over time.

Of major concern with the high nicotine brands is that these brands are highly addictive, making it very difficult for consumers to quit even if they are suffering from health problems. Also, the higher nicotine brands have much higher levels of cancer-causing nitrosamines. In June 1994 the American Health Foundation was funded by the National Cancer Institute to assess nicotine and pH of commercial U.S. snuff brands. The study found that the starter brand Skoal Bandits has a low dose of nicotine and low pH. For the other brands tested, percent of nicotine did not vary but the pH did, rising from 7.2 in Skoal Long Cut, to 7.5 in Skoal Fine Cut, to 8.0 for Copenhagen. By adjusting the pH, the amount of free nicotine rises sharply from the starter brands to the high dose Copenhagen, thus confirming UST's graduation strategy. The Hermann Kruger tobacco company from Denmark sells smokeless tobacco in the U.S. under the brand name Oliver Twist, which comes in five strengths ranging from light to heavy. The lightest brand is called "Freshman" and according to the company's instructions, is "perfect for beginners." "Bitter" is the highest

19

strength brand and is for "Senior connoisseurs and experienced smokers."

UST is not the only oral snuff manufacturer to employ low nicotine starter products. The Pinkerton Tobacco Company, whose present company is the Swedish Tobacco Company, manufactures a low nicotine product called Renegades that is sold in Skoal Bandits-like teabag pouches and a high nicotine brand called Red Man oral snuff. The Conwood Company sells a low nicotine brand, Hawken and high nicotine brand, Kodiak.

ADVERTISING AND PROMOTION OF STARTER BRANDS

The only products free sampled by UST are low nicotine brands Skoal Bandits, and Mint and Cherry Skoal Long Cut. Cherry is a flavor which is particularly appealing to young people because of the sweet taste. Oral snuff manufacturers promote and advertise starter brands through free sampling which is done through the mail, at sponsored events and in UST's College Marketing Program. During the last six months of 1984 over 400,000 samples were mailed in response to magazine ads. According to the Federal Trade Commission, 13% of all advertising and promotional expenditures went for free sampling in 1991 and 20% for public entertainment which included sponsored rodeos, auto racing, music concerts and other events where free sampling is routinely done.

According to National Leading Advertisers (NLA), advertising expenditures for the low nicotine brands far outweigh those for the higher nicotine brands. In 1983, total U.S. Tobacco advertising dollars for Skoal Bandits was 47% while the brand made up only 2% of market share by weight. Copenhagen, the highest nicotine brand, had only 1% of advertising expenditures but 50% of market share. UST spent $5.8 million in 1990-91 for print advertising for Skoal or Skoal Bandits. No advertising was reported for Copenhagen.

Advertisements for the low nicotine brands further support their role in the graduation strategy. The ads provide non-users instructions on how to use oral tobacco. A text for a Skoal Bandits brochure reads, "It's as easy as 1-2-3...All you do is put it in between your cheek and gum – the refreshing taste comes right through."

GREEN TOBACCO SICKNESS

Green tobacco sickness (GTS) is an illness resulting from dermal exposure to dissolved nicotine from wet tobacco leaves; it is characterized by nausea, vomiting, weakness, and dizziness and sometimes fluctuations in blood pressure or heart rate. On September 14, 1992, the Occupational Health Nurses in Agricultural Communities (OHNAC) project of Kentucky received reports of 27 cases of GTS. The cases occurred among tobacco harvesters who had sought treatment in several hospital emergency departments in south-central Kentucky during the preceding two weeks.

Morbidity and Mortality Weekly Report, April 9, 1993, Vol. 42, No. 13.

The UST ad campaign clearly shows the intent to promote experimentation with low nicotine starter products. UST manipulates nicotine bioavailability in their oral snuff brands and employs a graduation strategy based on free sampling of low nicotine among young males with no history of tobacco use. The marketing campaign has resulted in a surge in use among adolescent males.

Other nations that were recently faced with the introduction of oral snuff into markets, including Australia, New Zealand, Hong Kong and the European Community, banned the products. The long term impact on oral health and oral cancer from this campaign will be devastating unless something is done immediately. Based on this evidence submitted to the Subcommittee, oral snuff should be classified as a drug by the Food and Drug Administration.

READING

3

SMOKELESS TOBACCO INDUSTRY IS FALSELY INDICTED

U.S. Tobacco Company

U.S. Tobacco Company (USTC) is the largest American manufacturer of smokeless tobacco products in the United States. The following is a collection of responses to the inquiry of Congressman Harry Waxman of California.

■ POINTS TO CONSIDER

1. How does USTC respond in light of scientific evidence linking smokeless tobacco and oral cancer?

2. Discuss the author's statements involving nicotine manipulation. Does the author mention pH levels?

3. How does USTC refute the claims that a graduation process is used?

4. According to the company, what has been their history concerning minors and tobacco products?

Excerpted from U.S. Tobacco Company responses to the inquiry of Congressman Harry Waxman (D-CA) before the Subcommittee on Health and the Environment of the House of Representatives Committee on Energy and Commerce, November 29, 1994.

No step in USTC's manufacturing process is taken for the purpose of adjusting the nicotine level of its smokeless tobacco products.

THE CANCER QUESTION

In his testimony at the April 14, 1994 hearing, Mr. Taddeo (former President of U.S. Tobacco Company or USTC), expressed the Company's position that smokeless tobacco has not been established as a cause of oral cancer. This position, as to which the Subcommittee has asked for further explanation, is based upon the fact that, while a number of scientists believe that smokeless tobacco is a cause of oral cancer, others hold the view that it has not been scientifically established to be a cause of this disease.

Scientists on both sides of this controversy come from various scientific disciplines including epidemiology, toxicology, pathology and immunology. Their analyses and evaluations of the scientific evidence are influenced and shaped by their respective scientific disciplines.

NICOTINE LEVELS

The nicotine level in each of USTC's smokeless tobacco products is measured after the product has been packaged. USTA began taking these measurements in 1987 to comply with U.S. Department of Health and Human Services (HHS) nicotine reporting requirements pursuant to the Comprehensive Smokeless Tobacco Health Education Act of 1986.

In addition, other analytical measurements are taken from time to time, including moisture, grain size, pesticide residue, pH, organic acids, and nicotine at various stages, e.g., after leaf processing, during aging, after cutting, and during curing as part of a broad profile of data to assist the Company in understanding the manufacturing process. USTC does not believe these measurements provide sufficient information to determine with certainty at what point in the manufacturing process nicotine levels decline.

Differences in nicotine levels in USTC's smokeless tobacco products result primarily from the tobacco leaf blend. USTC's leaf blends are dictated by formulas that are decades old; Copenhagen, for example, is made using a formula dating back to 1822. Other factors, including moisture and flavoring levels, contribute to a decline in the nicotine level during the course of the manufacturing process. Even within an individual product containing a single formula and leaf blend, the nicotine levels vary from time to time (above or below the statistical mean) due to external factors such as different weather conditions affecting a particular crop year, or a particular growing region, and soil conditions. Indeed, the data underlying the statistical mean, collected by the Company since 1987 for government reporting purposes, indicates an overlap among the various products' respective nicotine levels.

FALSE ALLEGATIONS

Mr. Taddeo articulated the position of USTC as set forth in its statement of its current manufacturing practices: "U.S. Tobacco does not in any way manipulate or 'spike' the nicotine levels in its tobacco products. Nor does U.S. Tobacco take any action to control the nicotine content of its tobacco products before, during or after the manufacturing process." This statement was not intended to suggest that different blends of tobacco do not result in different nicotine levels.

USTC does not measure nicotine levels in unprocessed leaf, i.e., in tobacco leaf in the form it is received from the farmer, before or after purchase.

USTC does not restore nicotine at any point during the manufacturing process. The only material used in the manufacture of USTC's smokeless tobacco products, other than the tobacco itself, which contains nicotine, is denatured alcohol which is purchased from a supplier as a carrying agent for the application of certain flavorings that do not dissolve in water. The denatured alcohol (SDA-4) used by USTC has been denatured by its manufacturer with small amounts of nicotine. The use of nicotine as a denaturant for alcohol, which is to be used in the processing and manufacturing of tobacco products, is specifically approved by the Bureau of Alcohol, Tobacco and Firearms. The amount of nicotine that might be contributed to a USTC smokeless tobacco product through the use of denatured alcohol in the manufacturing process is so minuscule as to be unmeasurable by standard laboratory methodologies.

No step in USTC's manufacturing process is taken for the purpose of adjusting the nicotine level of its smokeless tobacco prod-

24

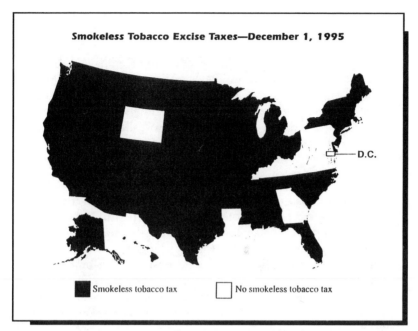

Smokeless Tobacco Excise Taxes—December 1, 1995

D.C.

■ Smokeless tobacco tax   □ No smokeless tobacco tax

Source: Center for Disease Control

ucts. It is known that nicotine levels decline as a result of the addition of water and other ingredients, and also to a minor degree due to evaporation.

USTC does not grow tobacco itself for use in its smokeless tobacco products, but instead purchases tobacco leaf both at open auction and from independent farmers who are members of various tobacco leaf associations. Tobacco field workers are employed by the tobacco farm owners, and are not under the supervision or control of USTC. Kentucky and Tennessee are the states where the tobacco used in USTC's smokeless tobacco products is cultivated.

GRADUATION HYPOTHESIS

The Company understands today that, in the early 1980s, there were discussions among some at USTC about a "graduation process," "hypothesis," or "theory." While the term "graduation process" apparently meant different things to different people, the theory seems to have been an attempt by some to provide a short-hand explanation for consumer behavior in switching between brands of smokeless tobacco, including between the Company's own brands.

The "fanciful concept" referenced in the Company's April 14, 1994, statement referred to allegations by Dr. Jack Henningfield that "graduation process" meant the Company employed a deliberate marketing strategy to entice consumers with low-nicotine products and then move them through so-called nicotine "addiction" to products with higher levels of nicotine. The Company never had such a strategy.

As best as the Company can now determine, the term "graduation process" as used in the early 1980s (i) did not relate to increasing levels of nicotine and pH; (ii) did not drive the Company's marketing strategies; and (iii) is contradicted by consumer behavior in the marketplace. Indeed, consumer demographic data demonstrate that there is significant brand loyalty among smokeless tobacco consumers, and that many – if not most – stay with the brand they first choose. Moreover, the data demonstrate that whatever brand switching occurs does not readily fall within any pattern that could be viewed as consistent with the notion of a pre-ordained "graduation process."

In addition to individual taste preferences, there are many social and other factors that cause smokeless tobacco consumers to choose their respective brands. The Company's current view on these issues was set forth in its statement of April 14, 1994: "Smokeless tobacco consumers remain loyal to a single brand or switch among a variety of brands according to their taste preferences, cut of tobacco, form and packaging."

CONSUMER SATISFACTION

The adults who choose to use smokeless tobacco products purchase brands they find satisfying according to their individual preferences, including flavor, cut of tobacco, form, ease of use, and packaging. In light of these obviously subjective preferences, it would appear that each smokeless tobacco consumer could define "tobacco satisfaction" differently. USTC first began using the slogans "Copenhagen, It Satisfies" and "It Satisfies" in 1939. Like many advertising slogans, the terms doubtless mean different things to different people.

HISTORY OF SMOKELESS TOBACCO

Smokeless tobacco was introduced in Europe early in the 16th century by explorers who found the natives in the Western Hemisphere using tobacco in several ways. Its use quickly grew in popularity throughout Europe and the British Isles. The use of smokeless tobacco has been a tradition in the United States since the 18th century, predating branded cigarettes by over a hundred years. Smokeless tobacco dominated the American tobacco market until the early 20th century when cigarettes and other lighted forms of the leaf began to win wide public acceptance.

Joseph Taddeo, former Chairman, U.S. Tobacco in Congressional testimony, April 14, 1994.

ADULTS ONLY

In 1986, and again in 1992 and 1993, the Company conducted market research which contained information on the age demographics of consumers of its smokeless tobacco products. The Company is producing this market research. According to the Company's most recent information, the age demographics of consumers of the Company's smokeless tobacco products are as follows:

USTC Smokeless Tobacco Product	Average Age
Copenhagen	34.91
Skoal Fine Cut	36.12
Skoal Long Cut	36.95
Skoal Bandits	37.51

USTC has for a number of years participated in an "adults only" policy program sponsored by the smokeless tobacco industry to promote understanding that use of smokeless tobacco products is a custom reserved for adults.

The "adults only" policy program is a national (as opposed to state by state) comprehensive public education campaign with one central purpose: to repeatedly and consistently communicate

27

our strict "adults only" policy to responsible adults nationwide. Our philosophy is that responsible adults are the people to whom youth look for guidance. Therefore, if these adults know and support our policy, we are making a difference.

Over the years, we have reached out to millions of adults – parents, educators, coaches, retailers, public officials, and law enforcement officers whom we feel have a special influence with youth. We have used public service announcements, such as "Smokeless Tobacco Is Not for Kids" and "Some Things Are Still for Adults Only" on television, in newspapers such as *USA Today*, and in magazines, to spread our message. We have communicated to adults through public addresses and specifically prepared literature on the subject. We have distributed hundreds of thousands of signs, buttons and cards to retailers across the country detailing our "adults only" policy and asking them to help enforce our policy.

TOBACCO EXCISE TAXES FOR TOBACCO YOUTH PROGRAMS

In addition to the efforts of USTC and the tobacco industry generally, tobacco excise taxes have been used by federal and state governments to enforce laws, including the minimum age laws for the purchase of tobacco products. Four states earmark revenue raised from excise taxes levied on cigarettes and/or other tobacco products (OTP) to fund, among other things, programs relating to tobacco use and youth. The four states are California, Idaho, Massachusetts and Washington. Tobacco excise taxes collected by both the federal and state governments are used to help enforce the law, including the minimum age of purchase law in a particular state.

For more than 130 years, the United States has levied a tax on tobacco products. During this period, more than $138 billion in tobacco taxes have been collected by the United States government. For the year ending June 30, 1993, the federal government received more than $5.6 billion from excise taxes on tobacco products, an increase of $500 million from the 1992 total tobacco tax collected of $5.1 billion.

CONTINUING EFFORTS

USTC will continue its efforts to discourage the sale of smokeless tobacco products to minors. To date, the smokeless tobacco industry has spent $1.35 million to communicate its "adults only" program. USTC also subscribes to the smokeless tobacco industry code confirming its long standing policy that eighteen years of age is the minimum age of purchase for smokeless tobacco products.

READING

4

THE DANGERS OF ENVIRONMENTAL TOBACCO SMOKE

Carol M. Browner

Carol M. Browner wrote the following statement in her capacity as the Administrator of the Environmental Protection Agency for President Bill Clinton's first administration.

■ POINTS TO CONSIDER

1. According to Browner, what was the most significant finding of the Environmental Protection Agency (EPA) Report on environmental tobacco smoke (ETS)?

2. Summarize the important findings of the EPA report, particularly with respect to ETS and children.

3. Discuss the various policy recommendations Browner outlines to reduce or eliminate ETS. Do you think these are feasible?

4. Why are some businesses afraid of "going smoke-free," according to Browner? Is this a reasonable objection? Explain.

Excerpted from the testimony of Carol M. Browner before the Subcommittee on Clean Air and Nuclear Regulation of the Senate Committee on Environment and Public Works, May 11, 1994.

Cigarettes don't just kill people who smoke. They also kill people who choose not to smoke. We have a responsibility to protect children and adults from involuntary exposure to other peoples' smoke.

Environmental tobacco smoke (ETS), also called secondhand smoke, is a mixture of the smoke given off by the burning end of a cigarette, pipe, or cigar and the smoke exhaled from the lungs of smokers. This mixture contains more than 4,000 substances, many of which are strong irritants, and more than 40 of which are known or suspected human carcinogens. Exposure to secondhand smoke is called involuntary smoking or passive smoking.

In January 1993, the Environmental Protection Agency (EPA) released an assessment of the respiratory health risks of passive smoking, titled "Respiratory Health Effects of Passive Smoking: Lung Cancer and Other Disorders." This report was issued under the authority of The Radon Gas and Indoor Air Quality Research Act of 1986, which directs EPA to conduct research and disseminate information on all aspects of indoor air quality. The report summarizes the findings of the Agency's comprehensive investigation of the respiratory health risks from exposure to ETS. It incorporates comments and recommendations from the public, as well as two reviews by EPA's Science Advisory Board, a panel of independent scientific experts in this field. The Science Advisory Board concurred in the methodologies employed and unanimously endorsed the conclusions of the report. The Department of Health and Human Services (HHS) has endorsed the report and the National Cancer Institute within HHS printed it as one of its series of scientific monographs.

Based on the total weight of the available scientific evidence, EPA concluded that the widespread exposure to secondhand smoke in the United States presents a serious and substantial public health risk.

FINDINGS OF THE EPA RISK ASSESSMENT

Perhaps the most significant conclusion of the report is the finding that environmental tobacco smoke is a human lung carcinogen, classified as a Group A carcinogen under EPA's carcinogen assessment scheme. This classification is reserved for those compounds or mixtures that have the strongest evidence of a cause-and-effect relationship in humans. Only 16 compounds have

31

received this designation. In the case of ETS, unlike any other compound the Agency has ever evaluated, we are able to see a consistent increase in human cancer risk at typical environmental levels, rather than extrapolating downward from very high occupational exposures, as we have had to do for such other Group A carcinogens as asbestos and benzene. Also, using these studies at typical environmental levels, EPA estimated that secondhand smoke is responsible for approximately 3,000 lung cancer deaths per year in non-smokers in the United States. Of these 3,000 annual lung cancer deaths, the EPA estimates that approximately 2,200 are attributable to exposure outside the home.

Environmental tobacco smoke causes other significant effects on the respiratory health of adult non-smokers. These include coughing, phlegm production, chest discomfort, and reduced lung function.

CHILDREN AT RISK

Although the finding that ETS is capable of causing lung cancer in healthy adults is extremely significant, I am personally very concerned about the very serious respiratory effects on young children – who are particularly sensitive to the effects of secondhand smoke – that are documented in our report.

Infants and young children whose parents smoke are at increased risk of lower respiratory tract infections such as pneumonia and bronchitis. In the risk assessment, EPA estimates that passive smoking is responsible for between 150,000 and 300,000 lower respiratory tract infections per year in infants and children under 18 months of age, resulting in between 7,500 and 15,000 hospitalizations each year.

Children who have been exposed to secondhand smoke are also more likely to have reduced lung function and symptoms of respiratory irritation such as cough, excess phlegm, and wheezing. In addition, passive smoking can lead to a buildup of fluid in the middle ear, the most common cause of hospitalization of children for an operation.

Asthmatic children are especially at risk. EPA estimates that exposure to environmental tobacco smoke increases the number of episodes and the severity of symptoms for between 200,000 and one million asthmatic children every year. Moreover, passive

smoking is a risk factor for the thousands of non-asthmatic children who develop the condition.

EPA's conclusions on the respiratory health effects of passive
smoking confirm and strengthen those of earlier assessments by
the U.S. Surgeon General (1986) and the National Research
Council of the National Academy of Sciences (1986). The
National Institute of Occupational Safety and Health (1991) concluded that occupational exposure to ETS causes increased risks
of lung cancer and probably heart disease. The position of the
National Cancer Institute (1993) is that ETS is a proven cause of
lung cancer in non-smoking adults and is associated with an
increased risk of coronary heart disease.

POLICY RECOMMENDATIONS

EPA firmly believes that the scientific evidence is sufficient to
warrant actions to protect people from involuntary exposure to
environmental tobacco smoke. Because of the health implications of exposure to ETS documented in our risk assessment, EPA
has recommended actions to help parents, decisionmakers, and
building occupants prevent involuntary exposure to secondhand
smoke. EPA's primary recommendations are that:

- Residents should not smoke in their home or permit others to do so.

- Every organization dealing with children – schools, day-care facilities, and other places where children spend time – should have a smoking policy that effectively protects children from exposure to environmental tobacco smoke.

- In the workplace, EPA recommends that every company have a smoking policy that effectively eliminates involuntary exposure to environmental tobacco smoke, either through complete bans or by limiting smoking to rooms that are specially designed to prevent smoke from escaping to other areas of the building.

- Employer-supported smoking cessation programs should be a part of any smoking policy.

- If smoking is permitted in a restaurant or bar, placement of smoking areas should take into account the ventilation characteristics of the space, to minimize involuntary exposure.

SECONDHAND SMOKE AWARENESS

EPA recently took part in a survey conducted in conjunction with the Conference of Radiation Control Program Directors (CRCPD), to assess the awareness of secondhand smoke and radon, as well as radon testing and mitigation rates, in the United States. More than 30,000 adults were surveyed about their knowledge of secondhand smoke. Ninety-five per cent of those surveyed had heard of secondhand smoke, and fully 86 percent of those believe it is unhealthy. Of the total sample, 82 percent say ETS is unhealthy, while only 9 percent disagree and say it has little or no effect on health. We believe the results of this survey can be extrapolated to the population as a whole. Indeed, according to a recent *New York Times/CBS News* survey of 1,215 adults, two-thirds of those responding to the poll favor a smoking ban in all public places.

EPA is working closely with public and private sector partners to continue to educate the public about secondhand smoke and actions that can protect people from the health risks associated with ETS exposure.

TOWARD A SMOKE FREE ENVIRONMENT

Many federal agencies, state and local governments and private sector organizations have begun to implement some form of smoking restrictions indoors as a result of the landmark reports issued in 1986 by the U.S. Surgeon General and the National Research Council of the National Academy of Sciences. Since publication of the EPA risk assessment on passive smoking, however, we have seen a rapid acceleration of measures to prevent involuntary exposure in a variety of settings, including workplaces, restaurants, sporting facilities, health and day-care facilities, shopping centers, and a wide range of other public facilities. It is estimated that about 23 percent of the U.S. population is effectively covered by restrictive smoking policies.

Despite this encouraging trend, there are many places where involuntary exposure to secondhand smoke still occurs. Many businesses are concerned about being left at a competitive disadvantage if they go smoke-free, or if their communities enact restrictive smoking ordinances and neighboring jurisdictions do not. While recent studies of the effects of local ordinances on revenues and the experiences of many businesses suggest that smoking restrictions do not reduce sales or revenues for businesses that choose to adopt them – in fact, many report increases in commerce and revenue – businesses frequently receive misinformation claiming that smoking restrictions will hurt their business.

CONCLUSION

Cigarettes don't just kill people who smoke. They also kill people who choose not to smoke. We have a responsibility to protect children and adults from involuntary exposure to other peoples' smoke.

READING

5

THE DANGERS OF BAD SCIENCE

Matthew Hoffman

Matthew Hoffman wrote the following article as adjunct policy analyst at the Competitive Enterprise Institute, a prominent conservative policy and research institute on public affairs in Washington, D.C.

■ POINTS TO CONSIDER

1. Why is Hoffman critical of the Environmental Protection Agency's (EPA) scientific standards in the environmental tobacco smoke (ETS) study? What is the ETS study?

2. Discuss the implications raised by Hoffman as a result of the EPA findings on secondhand smoke. What is the EPA?

3. What "ulterior motive" may the EPA have in promoting such findings about ETS, according to the author?

Matthew Hoffman, "EPA's Bad Science Mars ETS Report," **Human Events**, 13 Feb. 1993: 13, 18. Reprinted by permission from **Human Events**, 422 First Street, S.E., Washington, D.C. 20003.

The EPA's disregard for scientific standards threatens to open up American homes and offices to costly and intrusive regulations.

On January 7, 1993, the Environmental Protection Agency (EPA) announced the long-awaited results of its four-year study on the health effects of exposure to environmental tobacco smoke (ETS), better known as "secondhand smoke."

With all the rhetorical bombast that normally accompanies government pronouncements, the EPA called the results "absolutely unassailable from a scientific point of view." Not only does secondhand smoke cause cancer, proclaimed the EPA, it kills thousands every year.

LOWERING SCIENTIFIC STANDARDS

But the EPA's peremptory attitude notwithstanding, its study is hardly "unassailable." In fact, it appears that the EPA manipulated the study and lowered scientific standards to reach a politically desirable conclusion. The implications for both smokers and non-smokers could be devastating.

Instead of collecting new data for its study, the EPA relied on "meta-analysis," a technique that is controversial among scientists because of its potential for abuse. A meta-analysis pools the data from many smaller studies and reanalyzes them to achieve a more precise result. But researchers who selectively incorporate studies or fail to account for differences among the studies can significantly bias their findings.

The studies that EPA incorporated into its meta-analysis were not based on controlled, laboratory experiments on animals. The EPA arbitrarily excluded all such studies from its analysis, perhaps because none of them have ever found a connection between ETS and lung cancer.

Worse, the EPA violated a crucial scientific standard when it lowered the "confidence interval" (which is issued to interpret the results of a study) from 95 per cent to 90 per cent. If EPA's analysis had employed a 95 per cent confidence interval, as all of the studies it incorporated did, it would have found no connection between ETS and lung cancer!

37

NO BANS NEEDED

A review in 1993 examined measurements of air quality in 951 "smoking" and 905 "nonsmoking" homes. The average concentrations of respirable suspended particulates were 22 micrograms (millionths of a gram: there are 450 grams in a pound) per cubic meter (yard) for "nonsmoking" and 49 micrograms per cubic meter for "smoking", giving an average difference (that is presumably due to smoking) of 27 micrograms per cubic meter. A vanishingly small number.

The same review showed similarly small differences between "smoking" and "nonsmoking" offices, public buildings, restaurants and transportation. The reviewer then calculated the daily intake for the "maximally ETS-exposed person." This is someone who is exposed at home and while traveling, who works in a bar, and is also exposed in other public places. The value obtained was around 60 micrograms, per day. Now if one were to assume that ETS and mainstream smoke were the same (we know however that because of aging and dilution, they are very different), these numbers translate to about 1-4 cigarette-equivalents per year.

One of the basic tenets of toxicology is that "the dose makes the poison." All things are poisons, depending on the dose. Such tiny numbers as "micrograms per cubic meter" and "1-4 cigarettes per year" represent such trivial doses that it is scientifically implausible that they could result in meaningful toxicological activity. In fact, animals exposed at concentrations hundreds of times higher than those seen in homes and offices where smoking takes place show no meaningful changes at all. It is therefore inconceivable that public policy, calling for virtual bans on smoking, would be necessary to reduce exposure to such a negligible risk.

Dr. Chris Coggins in Congressional testimony, March 17, 1994. He spoke in his capacity as principal scientist for the R.J. Reynolds Tobacco Company.

DEVASTATING INTRUSION

The EPA's disregard for scientific standards threatens to open up American homes and offices to costly and intrusive regulations, and creates a precedent that might be used to indict other aspects of our living environment...

The new methodology of the EPA also promises a field day for plaintiff's attorneys, who stand to make billions suing employers, restaurant owners, even parents who exposed their children to ETS. Already, some attorneys speculate that smoking will soon be driven from homes and offices by the threat of devastating lawsuits.

Unfortunately, few voices have risen to challenge the EPA's flaunting of scientific standards. The tobacco industry's Tobacco Institute has been one of the few dissenting voices in the debate, and for obvious reasons it has been ignored as a tool of financial interests.

IMPARTIAL SOURCE?

However, the EPA should not be treated as an impartial source of scientific truth, because it has similar incentives to argue that ETS is a carcinogen. With every substance EPA classifies as cancer-causing, the agency increases its budget, gains power and prestige, and opens new vistas for its regulatory activities.

Perhaps most disturbing, the EPA's anti-smoker initiative represents a potential threat to individual liberty. Most Americans (including myself) don't smoke because we're unwilling to accept the risks, and we tend to applaud measures that suppress smoking, regardless of the rationale, because we think smoking brings risks no one should accept.

But the millions of Americans who do smoke are not imbeciles who need a paternalistic state to protect them from themselves. After decades of anti-smoking crusades and warning labels, smokers know the risks their habit entails and have decided to accept them.

Smoking is no more irrational than mountain-climbing or sky-diving; many recreational activities bring risks, and it should be up to the individual to assume them or avoid them. If we allow government bureaucracies to ban smoking because the majority thinks it's foolish, what is next?

THE FEASIBILITY OF A FIRE SAFE CIGARETTE: EXAMINING COUNTERPOINTS

This activity may be used as an individualized study guide for students in libraries and resource centers or as a discussion catalyst in small group and classroom discussions.

The Point: The production of a fire safe cigarette is possible

Lighted tobacco products, nearly all of them cigarettes – remain the #1 cause of fatal fires in the U.S. They account for roughly one of every five people killed by fire in the U.S. and roughly one of every four killed in a building or structure fire.

The Fire Safe Cigarette Act of 1990 initiated a series of studies to confirm the feasibility of a standard test, suitable for routine use, of the ignition propensity of a cigarette and to confirm that the physical properties of cigarettes found to correlate with ignition propensity in the laboratory were also correlated with fire risk in the real world.

In August 1993, The National Fire Protection Association's (NFPA) special study of the latter question concluded that "modeling showed four cigarette characteristics to be significant – filter, filter length, porosity, and pack type. Filter, filter length and

40

porosity all affect air intake, which therefore appears to be an important physical element in the combustion process associated with risk." The U.S. Consumer Product Safety Commission (CPSC), as the lead agency coordinating the series of studies, was responsible for assessing what all the studies meant, and they stated in their overview report, "The Commission shares the National Institute of Standards and Technology's (NIST) and the Technical Advisory Group's conclusion that the research during the present study, together with research undertaken from 1984 to 1987, establishes the validity and reliability of their test method within reasonable limits." CPSC therefore concluded that "it is practicable to develop a performance standard to reduce cigarette ignition propensity," which would include the test method and other elements such as acceptance criteria. In other words, if we as a nation choose to reduce cigarette ignition propensity, the tools are there to do so.

(Dr. John J.Hall, Jr., Assistant Vice President, Fire Analysis and Research, National Fire Protection Association)

The Counterpoint: Efforts to create a consumer-acceptable fire safe cigarette have failed

Despite our continuing efforts, we have not successfully developed a cigarette that consumers find acceptable and that is less likely to start fires in real-world situations if carelessly handled. There are two reasons for our lack of success:

1. The modifications to cigarettes to make them less likely to ignite other materials also make those cigarettes unacceptable to smokers.

2. Our product development is hampered by the lack of a test method that can predict what will happen if a cigarette is dropped on actual home furnishings in real-world circumstances.

Our efforts to develop a consumer-acceptable lower ignition propensity cigarette have not ended. Our work so far, though, has demonstrated the complexity of this problem. And that problem is compounded by the lack of a test method with real-world predictive capabilities. We will continue to work on both cigarette and test method development.

Reynolds Tobacco has worked for decades to develop low ignition propensity cigarettes. Early efforts focused on cigarettes with fire stops or other design characteristics that caused the cigarette to "self-extinguish." Consumers, however, demand products that do not have to be continuously re-lighted. Moreover, it also became apparent that just because a cigarette would extinguish within a certain period of time did not mean that it would ignite other combustible material before extinguishing itself.

We also conducted extensive patent reviews and evaluated the feasibility of inventions described in dozens of patents. Many, if not most, of these patents describe outlandish and unworkable ideas. Inventors, for example, have proposed encasing cigarettes in everything from clay to milk solids to asbestos. Over the years, we have also worked with our suppliers, especially paper suppliers, to determine what products, if any, might be available to affect ignition propensity, yet retain consumer acceptance. Those efforts have not proven fruitful.

[R.J. Reynolds Tobacco Company]

Guidelines

Examine the counterpoints above and then consider the following questions:

1. Do you agree more with the point or counterpoint? Why?

2. Why does Dr. Hall have an interest in promoting the point?

3. Why does R.J. Reynolds have an interest in promoting the counterpoint?

CHAPTER 2

HOOKED ON SMOKING

READING

6

NICOTINE IS AN ADDICTIVE DRUG

C. Everett Koop

C. Everett Koop, M.D., Sc.D. served as Surgeon General of the United States during the Reagan Administration. The following statement prefaces the 20th report of the Surgeon General on tobacco, released in 1988.

■ POINTS TO CONSIDER

1. Discuss how nicotine in tobacco products can qualify as an addictive substance. How powerful is nicotine as an addictive substance according to Koop?

2. Why, does the Surgeon General suggest, are many skeptical about classifying nicotine as an addictive drug?

3. Summarize the various treatment and public health strategies aimed at reducing nicotine addiction.

Excerpted from the preface to the Report of Surgeon General C. Everett Koop, 1988.

Cigarettes and other forms of tobacco are addicting in the same sense as are drugs such as heroin and cocaine.

This Report of the Surgeon General is the U.S. Public Health Service's 20th report on the health consequences of tobacco use and the seventh issued during my tenure as Surgeon General. Eighteen reports have been released previously as part of the health consequences of smoking series; a report on the health consequences of using smokeless tobacco was released in 1986.

Previous reports have reviewed the medical and scientific evidence establishing the health effects of cigarette smoking and other forms of tobacco use. Tens of thousands of studies have documented that smoking causes lung cancer, other cancers, chronic obstructive lung disease, heart disease, complications of pregnancy, and several other adverse health effects.

This report explores in great detail another specific topic: nicotine addiction. Careful examination of the data makes it clear that cigarettes and other forms of tobacco are addicting. An extensive body of research has shown that nicotine is the drug in tobacco that causes addiction. Moreover, the processes that determine tobacco addiction are similar to those that determine addiction to drugs such as heroin and cocaine.

ACTIONS OF NICOTINE

All tobacco products contain substantial amounts of nicotine. Nicotine is absorbed readily from tobacco smoke in the lungs and from smokeless tobacco in the mouth or nose. Levels of nicotine in the blood are similar in magnitude in people using different forms of tobacco. Once in the blood stream, nicotine is rapidly distributed throughout the body.

Nicotine is a powerful pharmacologic agent that acts in a variety of ways at different sites in the body. After reaching the blood stream, nicotine enters the brain, interacts with specific receptors in brain tissue, and initiates metabolic and electrical activity in the brain. In addition, nicotine causes skeletal muscle relaxation and has cardiovascular and endocrine (i.e., hormonal) effects. Human and animal studies have shown that nicotine is the agent in tobacco that leads to addiction. The diversity and strength of its actions on the body are consistent with its role in causing addiction.

TOBACCO USE AS AN ADDICTION

Standard definitions of drug addiction have been adopted by various organizations including the World Heath Organization and the American Psychiatric Association. Although these definitions are not identical, they have in common several criteria for establishing a drug as addicting.

The central element among all forms of drug addiction is that the user's behavior is largely controlled by a psychoactive substance (i.e., a substance that produces transient alterations in mood that are primarily mediated by effects in the brain). There is often compulsive use of the drug despite damage to the individual or to society, and drug-seeking behavior can take precedence over other important priorities. The drug is "reinforcing" – that is, the pharmacologic activity of the drug is sufficiently rewarding to maintain self-administration. "Tolerance" is another aspect of drug addiction whereby a given dose of a drug produces less effect or increasing doses are required to achieve a specified intensity of response. Physical dependence on the drug can also occur, and is characterized by a withdrawal syndrome that usually accompanies drug abstinence. After cessation of drug use, there is a strong tendency to relapse.

Tobacco use and nicotine in particular meet all these criteria. The evidence for these findings is derived from animal studies as well as human observations. Leading national and international organizations, including the World Health Organization and the American Psychiatric Association, have recognized chronic tobacco use as a drug addiction.

Some people may have difficulty in accepting the notion that tobacco is addicting because it is a legal product. The word "addiction" is strongly associated with illegal drugs such as cocaine and heroin. However, as this report shows, the processes that determine tobacco addiction are similar to those that determine addiction to other drugs, including illegal drugs. In addition, some smokers may not believe that tobacco is addicting because of a reluctance to admit that one's behavior is largely controlled by a drug. On the other hand, most smokers admit that they would like to quit but have been unable to do so. Smokers who have repeatedly failed in their attempts to quit probably realize that smoking is more than just a simple habit.

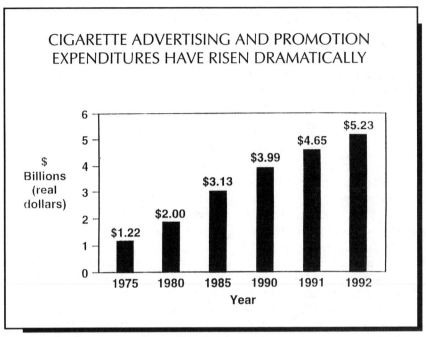

CIGARETTE ADVERTISING AND PROMOTION EXPENDITURES HAVE RISEN DRAMATICALLY

$ Billions (real dollars)

1975: $1.22
1980: $2.00
1985: $3.13
1990: $3.99
1991: $4.65
1992: $5.23

Year

Source: Federal Trade Commission

Many smokers have quit on their own ("spontaneous remission") and some smokers smoke only occasionally. However, spontaneous remission and occasional use also occur with the illicit drugs of addiction, and in no way disqualify a drug from being classified as addicting. Most narcotics users, for example, never progress beyond occasional use, and of those who do, approximately 30 percent spontaneously remit. Moreover, it seems plausible that spontaneous remitters are largely those who have either learned to deliver effective treatments to themselves or for whom environmental circumstances have fortuitously changed in such a way as to support drug cessation and abstinence.

TREATMENT

Like other addictions, tobacco use can be effectively treated. A wide variety of behavioral interventions have been used for many years, including aversion procedures (e.g., satiation, rapid smoking), relaxation training, coping skills training, stimulus control, and nicotine fading. In recognition of the important role that nicotine plays in maintaining tobacco use, nicotine replacement therapy is now available. Nicotine polacrilex gum has been shown in controlled trials to relieve withdrawal symptoms. In addition, some (but not all) studies have shown that nicotine gum, as an adjunct to behavioral interventions, increases smoking abstinence rates. In recent years, multicomponent interventions have been applied successfully to the treatment of tobacco addiction.

PUBLIC HEALTH STRATEGIES

The conclusion that cigarettes and other forms of tobacco are addicting has important implications for health professionals, educators, and policy-makers. In treating the tobacco user, health professionals must address the tenacious hold that nicotine has on the body. More effective interventions must be developed to counteract both the psychological and pharmacologic addictions that accompany tobacco use. More research is needed to evaluate how best to treat those with the strongest dependence on the drug. Treatment of tobacco addiction should be more widely available and should be considered at least as favorably by third-party payers as treatment of alcoholism and illicit drug addiction.

Public information campaigns should be developed to increase community awareness of the addictive nature of tobacco use. A health warning on addiction should be rotated with the other warnings now required on cigarette and smokeless tobacco packages and advertisements. Prevention of tobacco use should be included along with prevention of illicit drug use in comprehensive school health education curricula. Many children and adolescents who are experimenting with cigarettes and other forms of tobacco state that they do not intend to use tobacco in later years. They are unaware of, or underestimate, the strength of tobacco addiction. Because this addiction almost always begins during childhood or adolescence, children need to be warned as early as possible, and repeatedly warned through their teenage years, about the dangers of exposing themselves to nicotine.

Cigarettes and other forms of tobacco are addicting in the same sense as are drugs such as heroin and cocaine. Most adults view illegal drugs with scorn and express disapproval (if not outrage) at their sale and use. This Nation has mobilized enormous resources to wage a war on drugs – illicit drugs. We should also give priority to the one addiction that is killing more than 300,000 Americans each year.

NICOTINE ADDICTION

Although the epidemic of disease and death from smoking is played out in adulthood, it begins in childhood. Every day another 3000 young people become regular smokers. A person who has not started smoking as a teenager is unlikely ever to become a smoker. The tobacco industry has argued that the decision to smoke and to continue smoking is a free choice made by an adult, but nicotine addiction is really a condition that takes hold in young people...

Young people's addiction to nicotine is not limited to smoking. Many children also use smokeless tobacco, such as snuff and chewing tobacco. Of the 6 million people in this country who use smokeless tobacco, as many as 1 in 4 is under the age of 19 years...

Young people are the tobacco industry's primary source of new customers in this country, replacing adults who have either quit smoking or died. As the prevalence of smoking among adults in the United States has steadily declined, the prevalence among adolescents has remained unchanged or even increased slightly.

"Nicotine Addiction," **The New England Journal of Medicine**, July 20, 1995.

We as citizens, in concert with our elected officials, civic leaders, and public health officers, should establish appropriate public policies for how tobacco products are sold and distributed in our society. With the evidence that tobacco is addicting, is it appropriate for tobacco products to be sold through vending machines, which are easily accessible to children? Is it appropriate for free samples of tobacco products to be sent through the mail or distributed on public property, where verification of age is difficult if not impossible? Should the sale of tobacco be treated less seriously than the sale of alcoholic beverages, for which a specific license is required (and revoked for repeated sales to minors)?

In the face of overwhelming evidence that tobacco is addicting, policy-makers should address these questions without delay. To achieve our goal of a smoke-free society, we must give this problem the serious attention it deserves.

READING

7

NICOTINE CANNOT BE TERMED "ADDICTIVE"

Stephen M. Raffle

Stephen M. Raffle was a practicing psychiatrist in Oakland, California, when he made the following statement. At the University of California School of Medicine at San Francisco he served as Assistant Clinical Professor of Psychiatry for seventeen years and Assistant Clinical Professor of Orthopedic Surgery for ten years.

■ POINTS TO CONSIDER

1. According to Raffle, what have the studies on nicotine and addiction concluded?

2. How does the author compare nicotine use and illicit or "hard drug" use?

3. What conclusions does the author make concerning nicotine and addiction?

Excerpted from the testimony of Stephen M. Raffle before the Subcommittee on Health and Environment of the House of Representatives Committee on Energy and Commerce, June 23, 1994.

The message which has been consistently presented as the underlying rationale for regulation is that smokers become helpless addicted victims, the majority of whom cannot quit. This is flatly, patently wrong.

In the course of more than twenty years of clinical practice, I have evaluated and/or treated many patients with various drug addictions and drug intoxications. This includes heroin and other opiates, alcohol, amphetamines, barbiturates, and various forms of cocaine. Additionally, I have worked with many people with weight problems and other habitual and compulsive behaviors. Since 1990 I have served on my hospital's committee for chemically disabled physicians, and recently I was appointed to the Drug Diversion Committee by the California State Board of Podiatry for chemically disabled podiatrists. Thus, I bring to you the perspective of a teacher and clinician with considerable first-hand patient treatment experience.

RESEARCH REVIEW

As part of my professional continuing education, I have read extensively in the area of nicotine and addictive substances. I have read the following five documents titled: *Final Report on Project Hippo I, Report No. 1 Regarding Project Hippo II, Final Report on Project Hippo II, The Fate of Nicotine in the Body and A Tentative Hypothesis of Nicotine Addiction.*

In addition, I was provided approximately 40 research reports from the files of Brown and Williamson. These reports discuss research dealing with various aspects of human smoking behavior and nicotine pharmacology. Conclusions reported were summarized in a single sentence by the authors: "Our attempts to explain nicotine activities on brain functions on a bio-chemical basis was not successful."

NO CONCLUSIVE EVIDENCE OF ADDICTION

Heroin addicts, alcoholics, and other hard drug addicts are able to control their behavior when internally motivated. So are obese persons and smokers who choose to quit. The difference lies in the difficulty or price each must pay to achieve abstinence. With hard drugs, including alcohol, there is a profound and debilitating intoxication, severe physical and mental withdrawal and most importantly an overwhelming pattern of preoccupation with drug taking. In short, the entire lives of addicts are consumed with obtaining as much of their drug as possible and staying intoxicated. These individuals must make enormous life changes in order to successfully abstain. Their behavior patterns must be drastically altered and their social structure revolutionized in order for them to successfully rehabilitate. Smokers, obese persons, and coffee drinkers do not have the same burden in order to change their behavior. An honest objective assessment of these three groups inevitably results in the conclusion that they are fundamentally different.

NO COMPARISON TO "HARD DRUGS"

Smokers, coffee drinkers and obese persons share in common similar experiences of pleasure regarding taste, aroma, feel, anticipation and satisfaction. All of these experiences are mediated in the brain and elsewhere in the body at a molecular biochemical level. Psycho-active substances cause some of the pleasure in each of these behaviors. At no time is the user intoxicated, impaired or unable to control his actions. At all times individuals who are engaged in enjoying these activities can choose to modify them. If they do so, they will predictably experience the loss or alteration of a pleasurable activity, but they will not experience detoxification nor will it be necessary for them to radically change their social structure and behavior pattern. This means at no time will this group have to stop their usual daily activities, seek hospitalization, be in life-threatening situations, or experience profound physiological changes in their bodies as a consequence of abstention. This is not to minimize the power of ingrained patterns of behavior or the experience some people have in changing those behaviors. However, the quantitative and qualitative differences between addicts seeking to quit their addictions, and the second group, seeking to change their habits are profound. To include cigarette smokers in the group of drug addicts is a dishonest or ignorant mischaracterization of smoking behavior.

Both groups are nevertheless responsible for their behaviors. Addicts are not always intoxicated. Especially during periods of nonintoxication, they are capable of making the choice to bring their addiction under control. Persons with habits are always able to choose to change their behavior and successfully carry out their decision without extraordinary intervention and life-long treatment. The message which has been consistently presented as the underlying rationale for regulation is that smokers become help-

52

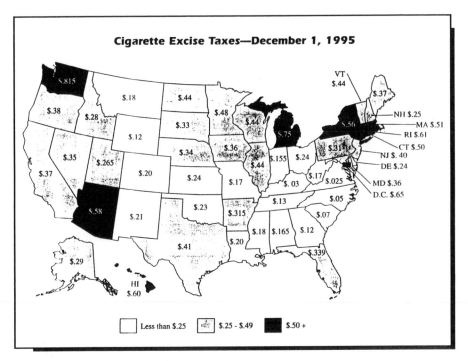

Cigarette Excise Taxes—December 1, 1995

$.815
$.18
$.44
VT $.44
$.37
$.38
$.28
$.48
NH $.25
$.33
$.44
$.56
MA $.51
$.12
$.75
RI $.61
$.35
$.34
$.36
CT $.50
$.265
$.155
$.24
$.31
NJ $. 40
$.37
$.20
$.44
DE $.24
$.24
$.17
$.17
$.025
MD $.36
$.58
$.03
D.C. $.65
$.23
$.13
$.05
$.21
$.315
$.07
$.18
$.165
$.12
$.41
$.20
$.339
$.29
HI $.60

□ Less than $.25   ▦ $.25 - $.49   ■ $.50 +

Source: Center for Disease Control

less addicted victims, the majority of whom cannot quit. This is flatly, patently wrong. At this time more people in America have quit smoking than are currently smoking and 90% to 95% of those people quit without medical intervention.

FURTHER RESEARCH

The 40 additional research reports I reviewed took a wide range of approaches to the study of smoking behavior and nicotine. Two of the largest projects, which were termed Project LIBRA and Project WHEAT, examined smoking motivation and behavior using questionnaires addressing many different psychological factors in smoking, including smokers' attitudes about anti-smoking information, their attitudes and behavior with respect to the issue of whether to quit or to continue smoking and their reasons for smoking. Other research examined chemical analytic studies of nicotine as well as how nicotine might influence certain physiological functions. Much of this was basic pharmacological measurement of cardiovascular and metabolic responses to nicotine; possible effects on the central nervous system were also examined.

53

SMOKING ENJOYMENT – NOT ADDICTION

I repeat, I do not believe that nicotine is addictive. I certainly believe that I am entitled to express my views even though they may differ from the opinions of others. My opinion is based on my common sense understanding of the major differences between tobacco and drugs in terms of the way people behave and how many people have been able to quit smoking.

To put the enjoyment of smoking cigarettes on the same level as addiction to drugs in my opinion defies common sense. If cigarettes were in fact addictive like cocaine and heroin, as is currently being asserted, there would be no way that 40 million American smokers would have been able to quit smoking, 90 percent of them with very little help at all, if any.

Excerpted from the testimony of Thomas E. Sandefur, Jr., former Chairman and CEO of Brown and Williamson Tobacco Corporation, before the Subcommittee on Health and the Environment of the House of Representatives Committee on Energy and Commerce, June 21, 1994.

Regarding the dispute about nicotine being addictive, I have several opinions regarding these specific papers: First, the scientific research reports reflect areas of study which were simultaneously being addressed and reported in the broader scientific literature. The papers did not reveal hidden proof of nicotine being addicting. Most of these studies replicated data that had already been published elsewhere. Second, the research did not address whether or not smoking or nicotine is addictive. Third, certain mild pharmacological effects were reported, but these were in context of narrow laboratory studies that do not tell us very much about smoking behavior in real life. Fourth, the most relevant aspects of reports, such as Project WHEAT, are those which actually collected psychological information on smoking behavior.

The authors examined the relationship between nicotine levels and cigarette choice. They replicated prior research about certain factors which enter into a smoker's decision to smoke. This decision-making framework was called "Inner Need" in the literature and so the same term was used in Project WHEAT. "Inner Need" did not refer to a physiologic need, physical craving, or uncontrollable drive but instead referred to such reasons for smoking as relaxing, watching TV, reading a book, etc. This study demonstrated that "Inner Need" showed no relationship with the nicotine delivery of the brand usually smoked. The data themselves actually demonstrate multiple reasons for smoking. They also spoke to a "requirement" for nicotine which refers to the test subjects' preference for certain levels of nicotine in the same cigarettes. The "requirement" varied greatly among the test subjects and was not linked to any physiologic effects of nicotine. While these data show that nicotine is an important aspect of smoking, they also reveal that, unlike addicting drugs but like coffee, taste, aroma and satisfaction are also considered to be determining factors.

When I compare this additional information to my clinical experience with drug addicts, it reemphasizes my conclusion that it is inappropriate and unwarranted to consider smokers as addicts.

THE TOBACCO INDUSTRY MANIPULATES NICOTINE

David A. Kessler

David A. Kessler, M.D. wrote the following comments as Commissioner of the Food and Drug Administration (FDA). In August 1995 under the leadership of Dr. Kessler and the Clinton Administration, the FDA released a series of regulation proposals targeted at curbing youth tobacco use.

■ POINTS TO CONSIDER

1. Discuss the issue of nicotine manipulation. Why is it pertinent to the tobacco regulation debate?

2. Summarize the evidence Kessler presents concerning genetic manipulation of nicotine.

3. Summarize the evidence Kessler presents concerning chemical manipulation of nicotine.

4. How does the reading characterize the tobacco industry?

5. What impact do you think information like this has on the national tobacco debate?

Excerpted from the testimony of David A. Kessler before the Subcommittee on Health and the Environment of the House of Representatives Committee on Energy and Commerce, June 21, 1994.

Over the last decade, nicotine levels have not dropped in parallel with tar levels – in fact, they have risen.

On March 25, 1994, I raised the question of whether the Food and Drug Administration should regulate nicotine-containing cigarettes as drugs under the Federal Food, Drug, and Cosmetic Act. A product is a drug if its manufacturer intends it to be used to affect the structure or function of the body.

Let me begin by summarizing the information that I presented. I reviewed the evidence that supports the scientific consensus that nicotine is addictive. I also reviewed the evidence we had at that time on the ability of the tobacco industry to control nicotine levels, including numerous industry patents for technologies to manipulate and control nicotine content. I described activities of the cigarette industry that resemble those of pharmaceutical manufacturers. I presented information that raised the question of whether tobaccos were blended to manipulate and control nicotine levels. And I provided data showing that over the last decade, nicotine levels have not dropped in parallel with tar levels – in fact, they have risen.

We have continued to focus our analysis and investigation on the physiological and pharmacological effects of nicotine and on the degree to which cigarette companies manipulate and control the level of nicotine in their products. The information that I presented about industry control and manipulation of nicotine the last time I testified before you was suggestive. Today I am going to provide you with actual instances of control and manipulation of nicotine by some in the tobacco industry that have been uncovered through painstaking investigational work.

I want to discuss two examples of nicotine manipulation in some detail. First, we have discovered the deliberate genetic manipulation of the nicotine content in a tobacco plant. It is the story of how an American tobacco company spent more than a decade quietly developing a high-nicotine tobacco plant, growing it in Central and South America, and using it in American cigarettes. Second, I will discuss how chemical compounds are added to cigarettes to manipulate nicotine delivery.

57

GENETIC MANIPULATION OF NICOTINE CONTENT

The project I am going to tell you about led to development of a tobacco plant code – named "Y-1." It has been an enormous task to piece together the picture of Y-1. Confidentiality agreements have made getting the facts very difficult.

The story begins in Portuguese with our discovery of a Brazilian patent for a new variety of a flue-cured tobacco plant. One sentence of its English translation caught our eye. "The nicotine content of the leaf of this variety is usually higher than approximately 6% by weight...which is significantly higher than any normal variety of tobacco grown commercially."

Prior to our discovery of the patent, an industry executive had told us that "flue-cured tobacco naturally contains 2.5 to 3.5 percent nicotine." Thus, this new specially bred plant would contain approximately twice the nicotine that naturally occurs in flue-cured tobacco. The holder of the Brazilian Y-1 patent was Brown & Williamson Tobacco Corporation, maker of such cigarettes as Kool, Viceroy, Richland, Barclay, and Raleigh.

Let me tell you why this discovery interested us. Industry representatives have repeatedly stated for the public record that they do not manipulate nicotine levels in cigarettes. The plant described in this patent represents a dramatic attempt to manipulate nicotine. Moreover, when we asked company officials whether plants were bred specifically for higher nicotine content, we were told that this was not feasible. We were told that tobacco growers and cigarette manufacturers have an agreement that the nicotine level of new varieties of tobacco grown in the United States can vary only slightly from the levels of standard varieties. Under this agreement, a new high-nicotine tobacco plant that varied more than slightly from the standard variety could not be commercially grown by farmers in the United States.

In 1977, Dr. James F. Chaplin had been working on genetically breeding tobacco plants with varying nicotine levels. In a 1977 paper, Dr. Chaplin indicated that tobacco could be bred to increase nicotine levels, specifically by cross-breeding commercial varieties of tobacco with *Nicotiana rustica*. *N. rustica* is a wild variety, very high in nicotine, but not used commercially in cigarettes because it is considered too harsh.

Dr. Chaplin has told us that his specially bred plants were not commercially viable because they did not grow well and literally did not stand up in the field. Furthermore, he was surprised that he could not get the nicotine levels as high as he anticipated. In fact, in his 1977 paper, the highest nicotine level he reported in these specially bred lines was 3.4 percent total nicotine, within the normal range for flue-cured tobacco. At the same time, international efforts focused on controlling and manipulating nicotine by alternative methods.

Over the next several years Dr. Chaplin continued his efforts to breed a tobacco plant with a higher nicotine level. During that time, an employee of a Brown & Williamson-affiliated company asked Dr. Chaplin for some of his seeds. Some of Dr. Chaplin's original plant varieties were used as a basis for Brown & Williamson's work.

In 1983, Brown & Williamson contracted with DNA Plant Technology to work on tobacco breeding. Much of the developmental work on Y-1 took place in the laboratories, greenhouses, and fields owned by DNA Plant Technology. After he retired from USDA, in 1986, Brown & Williamson also hired Dr. Chaplin as a consultant to work on Y-1 and other projects. What was accomplished was the development of a tobacco plant with a high-nicotine content – about 6 percent – that grew well and could be used commercially.

The story of this high-nicotine plant continues in Rio Grande do Sul, Brazil. DNA Plant Technology and Dr. Chaplin both told us they saw Y-1 growing in Brazil in the 1980's. These farms were under contract to Souza Cruz Overseas, a sister company of Brown & Williamson.

We learned that the U.S. patent application had been rejected by the patent examiner, but that Brown & Williamson had filed an appeal on February 28, 1994. However, two weeks later, on March 16, 1994, before receiving a response to their appeal, Brown & Williamson expressly abandoned the patent. On Friday, June 10, 1994, DNA Plant Technology told us that it had been authorized by Brown & Williamson to tell FDA that Y-1 was never commercialized.

On Friday, June 17, 1994, after our questioning of DNA Plant Technology, and following our letter to Brown & Williamson indicating that Brown & Williamson had not been cooperative with our investigation, Brown & Williamson told FDA that, in fact, three and a half to four million pounds of Y-1 tobacco are currently being stored in company warehouses in the United States. More significantly, Brown & Williamson revealed that Y-1 had, in fact, been commercialized.

Mr. Chairman, these brands of cigarettes – Viceroy King Size, Viceroy Lights King Size, Richland King Size, Richland Lights King Size, and Raleigh Lights King Size – were manufactured and distributed nationally in 1993 with a tobacco blend that contains approximately 10 percent of this genetically-bred high-nicotine tobacco called Y-1. When we asked company officials why they were originally interested in developing a high-nicotine variety of tobacco, they told FDA that they wanted to be able to reduce tar, while maintaining nicotine levels.

THE CHEMICAL MANIPULATION OF NICOTINE

Let me now move on to the second area. The six major American cigarette companies recently released a list of 599 ingredients added to tobacco. Nicotine is not one of the additives listed. But Mr. Chairman, a number of chemicals on that list increase the amount of nicotine that is delivered to the smoker.

Around the time the list was made public, a great deal of interest was directed toward substances on the list that sounded particularly toxic. Among those frequently mentioned was ammonia. Many people may have wondered why the cigarette industry would add ammonia to tobacco. In fact, there are many uses of ammonia. Our investigations have revealed an important one.

It is important to emphasize here that most of the nicotine in the average American cigarette is in the bound form. By that I mean it is not going to readily make its way to the smoker. This ammonia technology enables more nicotine to be delivered to the smoker than if the ammonia technology is not employed. Ammonia compounds known to be used include diammonium phosphate (DAP), ammonium hydroxide, and urea. In those countries, such as Germany, that do not allow DAP, other proprietary formulations are used.

One of the most common places the ammonia and ammonia-like compounds are applied is to reconstituted tobacco. When the cigarette is burned, the reconstituted tobacco serves as a source of ammonia in smoke. The amount of reconstituted tobacco can be as high as 25 percent of the tobacco in the cigarette. And we've seen ammonia compound levels as high as 10 percent in the reconstituted tobacco.

An experimental cigarette made of reconstituted tobacco treated with ammonia has almost double the nicotine transfer efficiency of tobacco. How widespread is ammonia use in the industry? The company handbook states that many U.S. tobacco companies use ammonia technologies. Until we have access to similar documents from other companies, we will not know whether other companies use it directly to affect nicotine levels.

To determine how well nicotine content is controlled in cigarettes, FDA laboratories compared the content uniformity of drugs in either tablets or capsules to the content uniformity of nicotine in cigarettes. What is striking is how little the nicotine content varies from cigarette to cigarette, suggesting tight and precise control of the amount of nicotine in cigarettes.

I have presented information on the control and manipulation of nicotine because I believe it raises certain important questions – questions that are even more important in light of the repeated assertions of the cigarette industry that it does not control or manipulate nicotine. Why spend a decade developing through genetic breeding a high-nicotine tobacco and adding that tobacco to cigarettes if you are not interested in controlling and manipulating nicotine? Why focus on the enhanced delivery of free nicotine to the smoker by chemical manipulation if you are not interested in controlling and manipulating nicotine?

THE GOALS OF CONTROL AND MANIPULATION

Why is there such interest in controlling and manipulating nicotine in cigarettes? Senior industry officials are aware that nicotine is the critical ingredient in cigarettes. Some in the industry have identified target levels of nicotine necessary to satisfy smokers' desire for nicotine. And the industry has undertaken research into nicotine's physiologic and pharmacologic effects.

Let me give you one example of how a company has identified specific levels of nicotine necessary to satisfy smokers and focused on how to achieve those levels. A company document describes consumer preference testing on "impact," which according to the company correlates with nicotine. The document states that impact is a "high priority" attribute of cigarettes and is: "...controllable to relatively fine tolerances by product development/product intervention...(by manipulating nicotine in blend/smoke...)"

This document goes on to describe an elaborate model for establishing the minimum and maximum nicotine levels tolerated by consumers. It states that the model provides "a median ideal point level for nicotine in smoke" for the population tested and a range of tolerable nicotine levels around this ideal point. Ask yourselves: Are these the kinds of studies that would be conducted by an industry interested only in the flavor or taste of nicotine?

READING

9

NICOTINE IS NOT MANIPULATED

William I. Campbell

William I. Campbell was formerly President and Chief Executive Officer of Philip Morris U.S. He presented this testimony before a House Subcommittee on Health and the Environment.

■ POINTS TO CONSIDER

1. What are the charges to which Campbell is responding?

2. According to the author, what has been the fate of nicotine levels in the past 40 years?

3. Discuss the author's response to the charge that Philip Morris manipulates nicotine levels. According to Campbell, when is nicotine monitored in the manufacturing process?

4. Does the author believe nicotine is addictive? Why or why not?

5. Does the author have faith in Federal Trade Commission (FTC) methods of monitoring nicotine? Why or why not?

Excerpted from the testimony of William I. Campbell before the Subcommittee on Health and the Environment of the House of Representatives Committee on Energy and Commerce, April 14, 1994.

Contrary to the claim that we are committed to maintaining, or even increasing, nicotine delivery in our products, the fact is that tar and nicotine levels have decreased dramatically over the past 40 years.

I would like to take this opportunity to set the record straight on charges that have recently been made against the industry and Philip Morris. First, Philip Morris does not add nicotine to our cigarettes. Second, Philip Morris does not "manipulate" or independently "control" the level of nicotine in our products. Third, Philip Morris has not used patented processes to increase or maintain nicotine levels. Fourth, cigarette smoking is not addictive. Fifth, Philip Morris has not hidden research which says that it is. And, finally, consumers are not misled by the published nicotine deliveries as measured by the FTC method.

The claim that cigarette smoking is addictive has been made for many years. The fact that tar and nicotine levels vary among our many products has been publicized for over 20 years. The process by which cigarettes are manufactured, and which, at our invitation, FDA representatives saw firsthand, has been publicly known for over 50 years. And the call for the FDA to assert, or be given, jurisdiction over cigarettes has been made and rejected by the FDA and the courts on several occasions in the past.

PHILIP MORRIS DOES NOT ADD NICOTINE TO OUR CIGARETTES

The claim that Philip Morris secretly adds nicotine during the manufacturing process to "keep smokers addicted" is a false and irresponsible charge. The processes used to manufacture cigarettes have been publicly disclosed for years in patents and the published literature. And the results of that processing – cigarettes with varying levels of tar and nicotine reflecting varying customer preferences – have been closely monitored and reported by the FTC, and the manufacturers themselves in every advertisement, for 25 years.

Contrary to the claim that we are committed to maintaining, or even increasing, nicotine delivery in our products, the fact is that tar and nicotine levels have decreased dramatically over the past 40 years. Today, the market is populated with a number of "ultra low" brands which deliver less than 5% of the tar and nicotine of popular brands 20 years ago.

Philip Morris and other manufacturers have reduced delivery in a number of ways. The most important is the use of increasingly efficient filters which substantially reduce many smoke components, including both tar and nicotine. Filtration reduces nicotine delivery 35% to 45% in today's brands, as compared to a "standard" cigarette made simply of tobacco and paper.

Through a process called ventilation, nicotine levels are reduced by 10% to 50%. Through the use of expanded tobacco – a process developed by Philip Morris, in which tobacco is "puffed" much like puffed rice cereal – tar and nicotine levels are reduced still further.

There has been a fair amount of recent discussion of the reconstituted tobacco process. Again, that process has been thoroughly described for years in the published literature. In that process, stems and small leaf parts are re-formed into a paper-like sheet. The reconstituted leaf process does not increase nicotine levels in tobacco or cigarettes. To the contrary, 20% to 25% of the nicotine in the tobacco used to make reconstituted leaf is lost and not replaced.

These processes, when combined in the cigarettes Philip Morris sells today, reduce nicotine delivery levels by more than 50% in the case of Marlboro, to 96% in the case of Merit Ultima, as compared to a "standard" cigarette made of nothing but tobacco and paper.

Ignoring these reductions, some critics have focused on minute amounts of nicotine that are found in tobacco extracts and denatured alcohol – which together have no measurable effect on nicotine delivery of our cigarettes. Philip Morris uses denatured alcohol to spray flavors on the tobacco. The alcohol is denatured – that is, it is made to taste bitter so that no one will drink it – under a formula required by the Bureau of Alcohol, Tobacco and Firearms (BATF) and found in the Federal Register.

Again, the small amount of nicotine found in denatured alcohol and tobacco extracts cannot be measured in cigarette smoke. The expenditure of millions of dollars to reduce tar and nicotine in these various ways undercuts any suggestion that Philip Morris is "intent" on adding nicotine to its cigarettes in an effort to "maintain" nicotine levels or to "addict" smokers.

PHILIP MORRIS DOES NOT "MANIPULATE" OR INDEPENDENTLY "CONTROL" THE LEVEL OF NICOTINE IN OUR PRODUCTS

The cigarette industry markets and advertises products by tar category to satisfy a variety of consumer preferences. Within tar categories, we attempt to provide a competitive advantage by providing the best possible taste. When creating a cigarette for a tar category, we select a particular tobacco blend and flavors to provide "uniqueness" for the product. The most significant parameters for determining tar delivery are the amount of expanded tobacco used, filtration efficiency, and ventilation.

So, how do we "manipulate" or independently "control" nicotine as our critics charge? The answer is we don't. We accept the nicotine levels that result from this process. As representatives of the FDA learned when, at our invitation, they recently visited our manufacturing center in Richmond, nicotine levels in tobacco are measured at only two points in the manufacturing process – at the stemmery, where tobacco leaves are prepared for processing, and then 18 months later after those leaves have been manufactured into finished cigarettes. Although Philip Morris maintains over 400 quality control checkpoints in the manufacturing process – for example, moisture levels, weight, etc. – none measures, reports or analyzes nicotine levels in tobacco.

PHILIP MORRIS HAS NOT USED PATENTED PROCESSES TO INCREASE OR MAINTAIN NICOTINE LEVELS

Commissioner Kessler spent a great deal of his recent testimony attempting to support the proposition that Philip Morris may be using secret patented processes to increase or maintain nicotine delivery in our cigarettes. We are not. The processes described in the patents referred to by Commissioner Kessler are not at all secret but, rather, were publicly disclosed years ago, first to the U.S. government and then to the world.

Philip Morris in fact has never used any of the processes described in these patents to increase, or even maintain, nicotine levels in any of its products. To the contrary, the only patents cited by Commissioner Kessler which Philip Morris has ever used were for the reduction and in some cases the virtual elimination of nicotine.

CIGARETTE SMOKING IS NOT ADDICTIVE

Many people like to smoke. Some people like the look and feel of the pack or the smell of tobacco. Some like to hold and fiddle with a cigarette. And, of course, there is the taste and aroma of the tobacco, and the sight of the smoke. Cigarettes contain nicotine because it occurs naturally in tobacco. Nicotine contributes to the taste of cigarettes and the pleasure of smoking. The presence of nicotine, however, does not make cigarettes a drug or smoking an addiction.

People can and do quit smoking. According to the 1988 Surgeon General's Report, there are over 40 million former smokers in the United States, and 90% of smokers quit on their own, without any outside help. Further, smoking is not intoxicating. No one gets drunk from cigarettes, and no one has said that smokers cannot function normally. Smoking does not impair judgment. No one is likely to be arrested for driving under the influence of cigarettes. In short, our customers enjoy smoking for many reasons. Smokers are not drug addicts.

CONSUMERS ARE NOT MISLED BY THE PUBLISHED NICOTINE DELIVERIES

All of the tests are conducted on cigarettes obtained from the marketplace. They are, therefore, the same cigarettes smoked by the consumer after all cigarette manufacturing processes have been completed. As a result of this testing, the nicotine delivery of all commercial cigarettes is measured and disclosed to the tenth of a milligram, both in public releases by the Federal Trade Commission (FTC) and, perhaps more importantly, in every cigarette advertisement.

Commissioner Kessler suggested that the FTC figures were misleading because smokers might "compensate" for lower tar and lower nicotine brands by smoking those cigarettes differently. In fact, the data indicates that, despite the dramatic reductions in tar and nicotine levels over the past decades, the number of cigarettes smoked by an individual has remained constant, and even declined slightly. More importantly, the data shows no difference in the number of cigarettes smoked by those who favor higher and lower yield brands.

READING THE DAILY NEWSPAPER

This activity may be used as an individualized study guide for students in libraries and resource centers or as a discussion catalyst in small group and classroom discussions.

One of the best sources for obtaining current information on social and political issues locally, nationwide, and globally is the daily newspaper. The skill to read with insight and understanding involves the ability to know where to look and how to "skim" the headlines for articles of interest. The best place to begin is the front section and the opinion/editorial pages. Other good sources include the sections on the economy and any special feature sections that are usually included in Sunday editions. Be sure not to overlook the sections that deal with local issues as they often contain stories of global concern that are happening in your own community.

Guidelines

Using newspapers from home or from your school or local library, skim the headlines and locate articles that deal with tobacco and nicotine addiction. With such a vociferous debate recently, between the tobacco industry and regulation advocates, today's headlines and editorials are a good source of information on the issues brought out in this anthology.

1. Try to locate several articles on the topic of nicotine addiction.

2. Do any of these articles discuss a "drug-like" or addictive nature (or lack thereof) concerning nicotine? If so, do they relate to any of the readings in the chapter?

3. Do any of the articles discuss how political shifts may enhance or color the debate on nicotine addiction?

4. Is the dialogue on nicotine addiction/manipulation important enough to gain national attention? Why or why not? Cite and explain those sources which brought you to your conclusion.

5. Explain why the issue of nicotine addiction, from the outside sources collected, has become important in the greater tobacco debate. How does this issue affect tobacco regulation or health care?

Other Projects

Start a scrapbook of articles, editorials, and political cartoons dealing with tobacco. Create a summary of the issues surrounding tobacco use, highlighting the issue of nicotine addiction/manipulation.

CHAPTER 3

THE REGULATION CONTROVERSY

READING

10

THE PROPOSED RULE: FDA REGULATION

Food and Drug Administration

The Food and Drug Administration (FDA) of the Department of Health and Human Services, introduced their proposals to regulate tobacco in August of 1995.

■ **POINTS TO CONSIDER**

1. Summarize the proposed rule.

2. Discuss why a federal agency feels the urgency to propose tobacco regulation.

3. What is the importance of advertising in tobacco regulation?

4. Discuss the objectives of "Healthy People 2000."

Food and Drug Administration, Health and Human Services, "Regulations Restricting the Sale and Distribution of Cigarettes and Smokeless Tobacco Products to Protect Children and Adolescents," **Federal Register**, vol. 60, no. 155, 11 Aug. 1995: 41314-16.

Although most segments of the American adult population have decreased their use of cigarettes, the prevalence of smoking by young people has failed to decline for more than a decade. Recently, smoking among young people has begun to rise.

The Food and Drug Administration (FDA) is proposing new regulations governing the sale and distribution of nicotine-containing cigarettes and smokeless tobacco products to children and adolescents in order to address the serious public health problems caused by the use of and addiction to these products. The proposed rule would reduce children's and adolescents' easy access to cigarettes and smokeless tobacco as well as significantly decrease the amount of positive imagery that makes these products so appealing to them. The proposed rule would not restrict the use of tobacco products by adults.

Specifically, the proposed rule would establish 18 years of age as the federal minimum age of purchase and would prohibit cigarette vending machines, free samples, mail-order sales, and self-service displays. It would also require that retailers comply with certain conditions regarding sales of tobacco, especially verification that the purchaser is at least 18 years of age, before a tobacco sale is made. Finally, the proposed rule would limit advertising and labeling to which children and adolescents are exposed to a text-only format; ban the sale or distribution of branded non-tobacco items such as hats and tee-shirts; restrict sponsorship of events to the corporate name only; and require manufacturers to establish and maintain a national public education campaign aimed at children and adolescents to counter the pervasive imagery and reduce the appeal created by decades of pro-tobacco messages, and thus help reduce young people's use of tobacco products.

The objective of the proposed rule is to meet the goal of the report "Healthy People 2000" by reducing roughly by half children's and adolescents' use of tobacco products. If this objective is not met within seven years of the date of publication of the final rule, the agency will take additional measures to help achieve the reduction in the use of tobacco products by young people. FDA is requesting comment regarding the type of additional measures that would be most effective.

SMOKING PROBLEM

Approximately 50 million Americans currently smoke cigarettes and another 6 million use smokeless tobacco products. These tobacco products are responsible for more than 400,000 deaths each year due to cancer, respiratory illnesses, heart disease, and other health problems. Cigarettes kill more Americans each year than acquired immune deficiency syndrome (AIDS), alcohol, car accidents, murders, suicides, illegal drugs, and fires combined. On average, smokers who die from a disease caused by smoking lose 12 to 15 years of life because of tobacco use.

In a separate document, FDA is addressing the issue of its jurisdiction over nicotine-containing cigarettes and smokeless tobacco products. The results of an extensive investigation and comprehensive legal analysis support a finding at this time that the nicotine in these products is a drug and that these products are nicotine-delivery devices within the meaning of the Federal Food, Drug, and Cosmetic Act. FDA proposes to regulate cigarettes and smokeless tobacco products by employing its restricted device authority, which affords the most appropriate and flexible mechanism for regulating the sale, distribution, and use of these products.

The primary objective of the proposed rule is to reduce the death and disease caused by tobacco products. Rather than banning tobacco products for the millions of Americans who are currently addicted to them, this regulation focuses on preventing future generations from developing an addiction to nicotine-containing tobacco products. In addition, the scientific evidence strongly suggests that nicotine addiction begins when most tobacco users are teenagers or younger and, thus, is a pediatric disease. Therefore, reducing the number of young people who regularly start to use tobacco products will help to prevent future generations of individuals from becoming addicted to nicotine.

The goal of the proposed rule is to help the country achieve one of the objectives of "Healthy People 2000," which is to reduce the number of children and adolescents who use tobacco products by roughly one half by the year 2000. The agency has modified the goal to include a different measurement tool and established seven years after publication of the final rule as the goal's endpoint. "Healthy People 2000" discussed national health promotion and disease prevention objectives in this country. It was

Cartoon by Richard Wright. Reprinted by permission.

facilitated by the Institute of Medicine of the National Academy of Sciences, with the help of the U.S. Public Health Service, and included almost 300 national membership organizations and all state health departments.

To determine the most appropriate regulatory measures, the agency reviewed the current patterns of use of tobacco products. According to the 1994 Surgeon General's Report, "Preventing Tobacco Use Among Young People: A Report of the Surgeon General," more than 3 million American adolescents currently smoke cigarettes and an additional 1 million adolescent males use smokeless tobacco. Every day, another 3,000 young people become regular smokers. U.S. data suggest that anyone who does not begin smoking in childhood or adolescence is unlikely to ever begin. Eighty-two percent of adults who ever smoked had their first cigarette before age 18, and more than half of them had already become regular smokers by that age. Moreover, the younger one begins to smoke, the more likely one is to become a heavy smoker.

Many young tobacco users become addicted to nicotine, a chemical substance in tobacco. Although they believe that they will not become addicted to nicotine or become long-term users of tobacco products, they often find themselves unable to quit smoking. In fact, among smokers aged 12-17 years, 70 percent already regret their decision to smoke and 66 percent state that they want to quit. Those who are able to quit experience relapse rates and withdrawal symptoms similar to those reported in adults.

Long-term addiction to nicotine can result in serious chronic diseases and premature death. An adolescent whose cigarette use continues into adulthood increases his or her risk of dying from cancer, cardiovascular disease, or lung disease. In addition, smokeless tobacco has been linked to oral cancer and other adverse effects. Although most segments of the American adult population have decreased their use of cigarettes, the prevalence of smoking by young people has failed to decline for more than a decade. Recently, smoking among young people has begun to rise.

READING

11

TOBACCO REGULATION MARKS THE RESURGENCE OF PROHIBITION

Mark Edward Lender

Mark Edward Lender is a professor and Director of Advanced Study and Research at Kean College of New Jersey. He is co-author of Drinking in America: A History, *and he has written widely on prohibition.*

■ POINTS TO CONSIDER

1. How does regulation of tobacco resemble the alcohol prohibition of the 1920s?

2. Discuss the underlying motives of social reformers that Lender suggests exist.

3. According to the author, why did prohibition fail? How does this relate to smoking?

4. What suggestions are given to curb tobacco use?

Mark Edward Lender, "Born Again: The Resurgence of American Prohibition," **The Freeman**. April 1996: 205-6. Reprinted by permission.

Prohibitionism is alive and well. In fact, the nation could be on its way to making some of the same mistakes it made during the 1920s.

Seventy-six years ago, America outlawed beverage alcohol. Initially popular, national Prohibition eventually collapsed amid a chorus of public resentment. The nation learned then what we know now: prohibition doesn't work. For all of its good intentions, prohibitionism is fatally flawed as public policy. It injects government into private lives. It makes criminals out of law-abiding citizens. And it tramples on our heritage of individual freedom and responsibility.

BACKDOOR PROHIBITION

Yet prohibitionism is alive and well. In fact, the nation could be on its way to making some of the same mistakes it made during the 1920s. This time the target isn't alcohol; it's tobacco. No one with any sense is calling for a constitutional amendment against smoking. But prohibition doesn't require such a drastic step. In 1920, when the nation voted for Prohibition, the majority of districts in America were already dry. Local option laws, temperance publicity, and tax policies had produced a *de facto* or "backdoor" prohibition in most of the country.

Similarly, smoking now faces "backdoor" prohibition. Restrictions on advertising, increasing bans on smoking, FDA efforts to regulate tobacco products, assaults on the tobacco industry, and abuses heaped on smokers all have the ring of the old crusade against Demon Rum.

RISK-FREE SOCIETY

Prohibition has never been just about drinking or smoking. Most reformers have wider social agendas. And the risk-free society some seem bent on creating today looks a lot like the perfectionist idealism of a century and more ago. Ardent drys were not content to mitigate problems; they wanted a nation fully cleansed of its "evils."

The same is true today, despite evidence that intrusive legal remedies are unnecessary. Drinking declined before Prohibition. Under the impact of temperance education, millions of Americans voluntarily gave up the bottle well before the first dry laws. Yet anti-liquor crusaders drove on, unwilling to tolerate any drinking. Today, the anti-smoking crusade persists despite declines in smok-

DRACONIAN RESTRICTIONS

In fact, politics rather than principle is almost certainly behind the Food and Drug Administration's proposed regulations to suppress smoking. Political crusades tend to be most successful when directed against an enemy. The Clinton Administration, having already run through the gamut of usual suspects – pharmaceutical companies, insurance firms, doctors, gun owners, government critics, talk show hosts, Republicans and religious activists, to name just a few – is now attempting to demonize the tobacco industry.

To be sure, the tobacco giants, by selling products that kill, make easy targets. Nevertheless, fundamental issues of principle are at stake. Draconian federal restrictions on smoking would simultaneously violate Americans' liberties and prove to be unworkable.

Doug Bandow, "Democratic Hypocrisy," **Copley News Service**, April, 1996.

ing. Since the 1964 Surgeon General's Report, perhaps 40 million or more have quit. But the legal quest for social perfection continues; voluntary choice doesn't suit the reform mentality.

Unfortunately, prohibitionism has degraded public discourse. Zealous to eliminate drinking, drys eventually demonized drinkers. The current anti-tobacco movement has targeted smokers for similar treatment. The matter goes well beyond forcing smokers to huddle in doorways; it has struck at the ability of the nation to conduct a civil public policy debate.

EXAGGERATED ADDICTION

All too often reformers have let advocacy outrun evidence. Their claims of addiction are a case in point. Temperance zealots insisted that all drinking led to addiction. This was obvious nonsense, and the public ultimately called them on it. Similarly many smokers may find it hard to quit, but millions have quit. Exaggerated claims of addiction are the rhetoric of a movement determined on victory at all costs.

How far will the logic of prohibition extend? Using arguments similar to those employed against drinking and smoking, a few social critics already have targeted strong perfumes because they offend others or trigger allergies. Some would tax low-nutrition foods because those who eat them could pose a burden on the health-care system.

The implications of these prohibitionist initiatives are staggering. Heart disease remains America's greatest killer, so should we tax beef or eggs because of their cholesterol content? Do we ban suntanning because it causes cancer? Or any other personal behavior because someone else has determined that it is not good for us?

DISAPPOINTING RESULTS

However well-meaning its goals, the results of prohibition have been disappointing. In the early 1920s, national Prohibition posted only short-term successes in reducing drinking and alcohol-related problems. Illegal markets grew steadily. Consumption levels climbed. So did disrespect for the law and the corruption of law enforcement.

Severe anti-tobacco regulations could lead to the same kinds of trouble. It is clear that illegal markets will fill any void created through cigarette bans. In 1993, for example, Canada imposed draconian cigarette taxes in an effort to discourage smoking. Smugglers were soon supplying about one-third of all Canadian cigarette sales. Michigan tried to tax tobacco into extinction a year later and saw citizens turn to bootlegged products. Moreover, serious First Amendment issues have arisen from efforts to curb tobacco advertising. Unreasonable legal and regulatory attacks on behavior as personal as smoking and drinking have caused at least as many problems as they have solved.

Clearly the excesses of prohibitionism are unnecessary. Today, the public is served well through educational campaigns. These are noncoercive and they work: witness the dramatic decline in smoking after 1964. Furthermore, all states and many cities have laws against tobacco sales to children. These should be enforced. The consistent application of such laws does not inhibit the free choice of adults. Yet it may serve to eliminate an emotional propaganda theme among anti-tobacco zealots.

America is a democracy and Americans can obviously ban behavior that they find objectionable. They have in the past. They may again. Before they do, they should be aware of the damaging implications of banning tobacco. And we all should be honest enough to call it what it is – prohibition.

READING

12

ADVERTISING RESTRICTION IS NEEDED

Bill Clinton

President Bill Clinton delivered the following address from the Rose Garden in the White House to announce the new Food and Drug Administration regulations on children and tobacco.

■ **POINTS TO CONSIDER**

1. Discuss why Bill Clinton decided to create a proposal for tobacco regulation.

2. How does the President describe the role of tobacco advertising?

3. What are the human and economic costs of smoking?

4. Summarize the specific regulations on children and tobacco.

President Bill Clinton in a Rose Garden address to the nation from the White House, 23 Aug. 1995.

This epidemic is no accident. Children are bombarded daily by massive marketing campaigns.

Today we are taking direct action to protect our children from tobacco and especially from the advertising that hooks children on a product. I hear from time to time politicians say that they don't really think advertising has much to do with it. And whenever I hear one say that I say, well, how come we're all spending so much money advertising when we run for office then? If it's immaterial, let's just pull it all off and see what happens to us.

Cigarette smoking is the most significant public health problem facing our people. More Americans die every year from smoking related diseases than from AIDS, car accidents, murders, suicides and fires combined. The human cost doesn't begin to calculate the economic costs – the thing that galvanized the legal claims of the Attorney Generals, the absolutely staggering burdens on the American health care system and on our economy in general.

But make no mistake about it, the human cost is by far the most important issue. For every day, even though it's illegal, 3,000 of our young people start smoking, and 1,000 of them will die earlier than they would otherwise as a result. The vast majority of people who smoke in America today started when they were teenagers. If they don't start smoking when they're on a schoolyard, it's very likely they never will.

EPIDEMIC

This epidemic is no accident. Children are bombarded daily by massive marketing campaigns that play on their vulnerabilities, their insecurities, their longings to be something in the world. Joe Camel promises that smoking will make you cool. Virginia Slims models whisper that smoking will help you stay thin. T-shirts and sports sponsorships sends the message that healthy and vigorous people smoke and that smoking is fun.

A year ago, we launched a comprehensive strategy to kick tobacco out of the lives of our children. We proposed strong restrictions on advertising, marketing and sales of cigarettes to children. In the year that followed, the FDA received a torrent of comments from the public – more than 700,000 – by far the largest outpouring of public response in the FDA's history. The FDA has heard from doctors, scientists, tobacco companies and

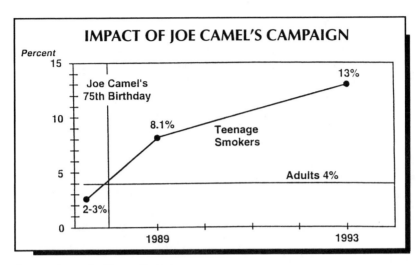

IMPACT OF JOE CAMEL'S CAMPAIGN

Percent

Joe Camel's 75th Birthday

8.1%

Teenage Smokers

13%

Adults 4%

2-3%

1989   1993

Source: Center for Disease Control

tens of thousands of children. We have carefully considered the evidence. It is clear that the action being taken today is the right thing to do, scientifically, legally, and morally.

So today we are acting. **First**, young people will have to prove their age with an ID to buy cigarettes. **Second**, cigarette vending machines will be banned from anywhere children and teenagers can go. **Third**, children will be free of tobacco advertising on bill-boards near their schools and playgrounds, and billboards in other locations will be restricted to black and white, text-only messages. **Fourth**, if a tobacco ad is in a publication children and teenagers are likely to read, it also has to be black and white with no pic-tures. **Fifth**, companies will no longer be permitted to target young people with marketing gimmicks like T-shirts and gym bags. **Sixth**, cigarette companies may no longer use brand names to sponsor tennis tournaments, auto races and other sporting events. **Finally**, the FDA will soon take steps to require the tobac-co industry to educate our children about the real dangers of smoking. There is abundant evidence of these troubling trends and a lot of young people simply don't believe there's any risks to their health.

83

CHILDREN

With this historic action we are taking today, Joe Camel and the Marlboro Man will be out of our children's reach forever. I want to be clear – we've said it before, let's say it again – cigarettes are a legal product for adults. They have a perfect right to decide whether to smoke. There are many, many good people who have been farming and growing tobacco for generations in their families. They have a right to make a living for themselves and their families, and they will continue to do so. But let's be honest: we hope that over the long run, if we can dramatically reduce rates of smoking among children, the overall consumption of cigarettes will decline. If that happens, these good people who farmed the land and worked hard should not be left behind. And all of us who have sought this course have a responsibility to help them if they face difficulties.

The cigarette companies still have a right to market their products to adults. But today we are drawing the line on children, fulfilling our obligation as adults to protect them from influences that too often are stronger than they are.

As I said before, I want to say again, this action is a tribute to so many of you who are here today. It is a tribute to the parents, the teachers, the doctors, and the public officials. Dr. Bristow, I particularly want to commend the American Medical Association (AMA) for its writings in its journal, and its relentless efforts to educate the American people through the physicians of this country. But I'd like to pay special tribute to the children of America who have joined this crusade, who have organized and led a massive grass-roots movement throughout America to educate and inform people about the dangers of tobacco smoking for children.

They've staged teach-ins and "Kick Butts" days all across the country. They have used positive peer pressure on people who could care less what a lot of us old fogies think, to teach their fellow students that smoking is not cool. So I want to thank these children for the work they have done to save their generation.

CONCLUSION

A lot of the work we do around here we know will only be fully manifest in people's lives in the future. We know we can't guarantee the success of any individual or family, but we have to guarantee them the tools and conditions that will enable them to make

ADVERTISING

Teenagers are three times more sensitive to cigarette advertising than adults, according to a new study published today in the American Marketing Association's *Journal of Marketing.* The study examined advertising expenditures between 1974 and 1993 for nine different cigarette brands and the resulting sales of cigarettes to 12-to-18-year-old and adult smokers. It is the first study to examine the relationship between the intensity of cigarette advertising and the resulting brand market shares among adults versus youth.

The study, which relied on market share modeling and analysis to reach its conclusions, found that when cigarette marketers change the rate of cigarette advertising, the impact is far more dramatic among teens.

"This study has conclusively shown for the first time that cigarette advertising has a much greater impact on teens than on adults," said Richard W. Pollay, lead author of the study. Pollay is professor of marketing and curator of the History of Advertising Archives at the University of British Columbia in Vancouver, Canada. "The study finds that when cigarette marketers increase the amount of advertising for particular brands, the corresponding sales of these cigarettes go up. But the main action in the marketplace is among youth smokers, not among adults."

"Cigarette Advertising," *Campaign for Tobacco-Free Kids* Press Release, April 3, 1996.

the most of their own lives. Today we take a real step to make sure that they have those lives in full measure. We have today met our responsibility to help our country protect its values, protect its children, and ensure its future.

READING

13

TOBACCO ADVERTISING REGULATIONS AMOUNT TO CENSORSHIP

American Association of Advertising Agencies

The American Association of Advertising Agencies (AAAA) is the national association of the advertising agency business. Its members include more than 600 advertising agencies located in virtually every state in the U.S., with offices worldwide. AAAA agencies place some 80 percent of all national advertising and provide clients with a full range of marketing services.

■ POINTS TO CONSIDER

1. What problems do proposed tobacco advertising restrictions pose for organizations, journals, etc., that receive tobacco advertising money?

2. Discuss the issue of censorship. Why does the reading contend that the restrictions effectively equal a "ban" on tobacco ads?

3. Into whose jurisdiction does the AAAA believe tobacco advertising falls and why?

Excerpted from "Comments of the AAAA in Opposition to Proposed Rules to Restrict the Advertising of Tobacco Products" submitted to the FDA by the American Association of Advertising Agencies.

Even for those Americans who personally oppose tobacco use, the blatant disregard for the Constitution and the American people evidenced by the proposed regulations should be alarming.

On August 10, 1995, with much fanfare, including a press conference at the White House, President Clinton and the leadership of the Department of Health and Human Services and the Food and Drug Administration (FDA) announced proposed regulations to govern the sale and distribution of nicotine-containing cigarettes and smokeless tobacco products. The next day, August 11, the proposed regulations, along with a lengthy written explanation of their purported justification, were released via special report in the *Federal Register.*

These comments are submitted by the American Association of Advertising Agencies, Inc. (AAAA) in strong opposition to the proposed regulations because they severely restrict – indeed, for all practical purposes, they effectively ban – the advertising of cigarettes and smokeless tobacco products. Imposition of that ban would be wrong, and would have numerous adverse consequences for the nation while failing to achieve the goals that the President and the FDA profess to seek.

INFORMATION CONTROL

Under the guise of concern for children and adolescents, the proposed advertising regulations ban truthful commercial speech about tobacco in an effort to "protect" American consumers from information that the FDA believes might be harmful. Such a blatant attempt to use "information control" to manipulate lawful behavior is antithetical to the principles of the U.S. Constitution. First, the FDA's unilateral assertion of regulatory authority clearly contradicts repeated directives of Congress as to how, when and by whom cigarette advertising should be regulated. In addition, the FDA regulations will not "directly advance" a "substantial" government interest which can be better served by "less restrictive" means, and thus they fail the well-established test for constitutionality under the First Amendment.

Finally, by usurping decision-making power from informed consumers and placing it into the hands of an unelected regulatory body, the regulations reflect contempt for consumers and their ability to discern what is best for them. Such an exercise of raw

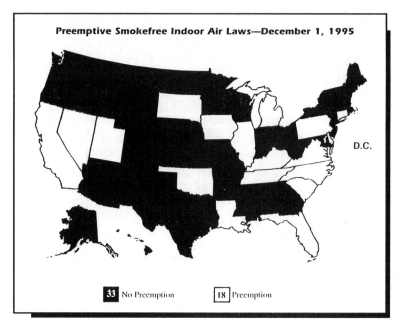

Preemptive Smokefree Indoor Air Laws—December 1, 1995

D.C.

33 No Preemption **18** Preemption

Source: Center for Disease Control

regulatory power is particularly unwelcome in an era when the majority of Americans want to reduce government intrusion into their lives. Even for those Americans who personally oppose tobacco use, the blatant disregard for the Constitution and the American people evidenced by the proposed regulations should be alarming. Censorship is habit-forming and, once established, can take on a life of its own.

BATTLING CENSORSHIP

Regardless of the diverse personal views on tobacco use, the collective view on tobacco advertising is more unified: the overwhelming professional consensus calls for continuing opposition to regulations, such as those the FDA now proposes, that would significantly restrict the right of advertisers and their agencies to communicate with the public. It is the censorship embodied in the proposed regulations that gives rise to these comments, not the controversial benefits or deficiencies of tobacco products themselves.

It has long been a fundamental policy of the AAAA to resist and oppose any initiative by any government entity to ban or restrict the truthful non-deceptive advertising of any legal product, no matter how controversial that product may be. Thus, while the AAAA takes no position on the merits of smoking *per se*, we strongly believe that protection of the right to advertise lawful products is an inherent component of free expression and a critical part of our nation's liberties. The proposed regulations must therefore be opposed not only to prevent direct injury to free speech in this particular context, but also to prevent future harms resulting from a regulatory "slippery slope," as assaults on speech in one context pave the way for assaults on speech in others.

SCOPE OF RESTRICTIONS

Constitutional jurisprudence demands that when evaluating First Amendment implications, a law "must be tested by its operation and effect." Near v. Minnesota, 283 U.S. 697 (1931). On the federal level, the Federal Cigarette Labeling and Advertising Act, 15 U.S.C. 1331 et seq., has for more than a quarter-century governed federal regulation of tobacco advertising, and, as amended, has banned cigarette advertising on television and radio; required cigarette packages and advertising to carry specified health warnings; and directed the Federal Trade Commission (FTC) to submit annually to Congress a report concerning cigarette advertising and promotion, along with any agency recommendations for additional legislation. The FTC has authority to address unfair or deceptive cigarette advertising under the Federal Trade Commission Act, and the agency has not hesitated to exercise that authority when circumstances have warranted. State and local restrictions also abound. In short, there exists today an established set of mechanisms to oversee and, if appropriate, to regulate the advertising of tobacco products to prevent consumer deception.

The FDA's proposed regulations would be imposed in addition to the mechanisms already established, but would effectively overrun the existing regulatory framework. The scope of the FDA's proposed regulations is virtually unlimited because the regulations specifically ban all advertising for tobacco products that is not expressly permitted by the FDA.

MISLEADING INFORMATION

This draconian regulatory system is warranted, according to the FDA Report, primarily because "tobacco products are among the most heavily advertised products in the United States." (FDA Report at 41315.) The Report asserts that each year almost $2 billion is spent on "advertising and promotion" of tobacco products. But the Report's handy compilation of data drastically overstates the magnitude of advertising expenditures. In fact, in 1993 (the most recent year of available data) only about one-fourth of the dollars the Report claims ($541 million) was spent on magazine, newspaper and billboard advertising; the bulk, more than a billion dollars, went not to advertising but to consumer purchase rebates, promotion allowances for retailers, coupons and other activities that are not advertising.

Moreover, when year-to-year trends are considered, the total of dollars spent on advertising of tobacco products has in fact fallen by more than 58% in only four years: from $834 million in 1990 to $541 million in 1993. That decrease in actual advertising expenditures occurred without any need for FDA intrusion and absolutely rebuts the notion of the FDA Report that tobacco advertising is so prevalent as to overwhelm our nation's youth.

In the face of this marked decline in advertising expenditures, the FDA proposes the most encompassing regulation of a mainstream product's advertising ever devised. The all-inclusive nature of the regulations can best be appreciated in the context of national magazines. The proposed regulations permit only "tombstone"-type black and white advertising in any magazine having more than 2 million young readers or 15% of its readership under age 18. While it is easy to envision *Boys Life* falling within those guidelines, it would be wrong to assume that the effects of the regulation will be limited only to magazines having an identifiable youthful readership. The fact is that many of the most recognized national magazines may also fall within the scope of that regulation.

There are many magazines that would be adversely impacted by the proposed regulations in their present form, although precise determinations will be very difficult given that few, if any, magazines compile specific information as to the ages of their subscribers, and no magazine is able to limit its total readership, including pass-along readers. The consequences to these magazines, and many others, will be severe and extreme because the proposed regulations will bring a virtual end to tobacco product print advertising.

The consequences of the FDA's proposed restrictions, when considered in their entirety, would be nothing short of a total ban on all advertising now used in connection with the lawful sale of tobacco products to adult consumers. Our society should not tolerate – and, as these Comments will demonstrate, the First Amendment does not permit – such a sweeping and paternalistic government effort to impose "better living through censorship."

WHAT IS EDITORIAL BIAS?

This activity may be used as an individualized study guide for students in libraries and resource centers or as a discussion catalyst in small group and classroom discussions.

The capacity to recognize an author's point of view is an essential reading skill. The skill to read with insight and understanding involves the ability to detect different kinds of opinions or bias. **Sex bias, race bias, ethnocentric bias, political bias**, and **religious bias** are five basic kinds of opinions expressed in editorials and all literature that attempts to persuade. They are briefly defined below.

Five Kinds of Editorial Opinion or Bias

Sex Bias – The expression of dislike for and/or feeling of superiority over the opposite sex or a particular sexual minority.

Race Bias – The expression of dislike for and/or feeling of superiority over a racial group.

Ethnocentric Bias – The expression of a belief that one's own group, race, religion, culture, or nation is superior. Ethnocentric persons judge others by their own standards and values.

Political Bias – The expression of political opinions and attitudes about domestic or foreign affairs.

Religious Bias – The expression of a religious belief or attitude.

Guidelines

1. From the readings in Chapter Three, locate five sentences that provide examples of editorial opinion or bias.

2. Write down the above sentences and determine what kind of bias each sentence represents. Is it **sex bias, race bias, ethnocentric bias, political bias** or **religious bias**.

3. Read through the following statements and decide which ones represent a form of **editorial bias**. Evaluate each statement by using the method indicated below:

- **Mark (S)** for any statements that reflect sex bias.
- **Mark (R)** for race bias.
- **Mark (E)** for ethnocentric bias.
- **Mark (P)** for political bias.
- **Mark (F)** for statements that are factual.

_____ 1. Restrictive tobacco regulations will lead to the same problems caused by Prohibition in the 1920s.

_____ 2. The tobacco industry has been seeking adolescent and young adult consumers to replace those who have died due to smoking-related illness.

_____ 3. Over 400,000 people in the United States die every year due to smoking-related illness.

_____ 4. The Joe Camel Campaign of R.J. Reynolds attracts children to cigarettes because of the flashy, upbeat cartoon character it features.

_____ 5. The marketing and promotional campaigns of the tobacco industry are only to convince adult smokers to switch current brands, not to solicit children.

_____ 6. Virtually all of the market for chewing tobacco is made up of male consumers.

_____ 7. The target market for Virginia Slims is women.

_____ 8. The most serious problem involving regulation concerns the First Amendment.

_____ 9. In an age of government downsizing, it is inappropriate for the federal government to propose burdensome regulations upon the tobacco industry.

_____ 10. The assault against the tobacco industry represents an overall anti-business message.

_____ 11. Black women tend to have lower rates of smoking than white women.

_____ 12. The pleasure of smoking is not only a sin, but a great health threat.

_____ 13. The anti-tobacco rhetoric is promulgated by left-wing zealots, who will ruin our prosperous nation if allowed to continue their attacks against a successful and profitable industry.

_____ 14. The anti-tobacco lobby is made of right-wing operatives who seek to punish those who smoke (particularly the poor, who have higher rates of smoking than the general population.)

_____ 15. The United States has a proud tradition with tobacco. Rather than regulating tobacco at home, the current administration should seek ways to promote the successful industry abroad (particularly in the emerging markets of Asia) and tear down trade barriers for tobacco abroad.

CHAPTER 4

LITIGATION, LIABILITY AND THE LAW

READING

14

TOBACCO INDUSTRY IS LIABLE FOR HEALTH CARE DAMAGES

The State of Minnesota

The State of Minnesota, under direction of Attorney General Hubert (Skip) Humphrey III, filed suit in August of 1994 against the seven major tobacco companies to reclaim Medicaid and other state health care costs incurred through tobacco-related illness. Blue Cross Blue Shield of Minnesota (BCBSM), the only non-profit health service plan provider in MN, originally filed as a co-defendant. Other states, including Florida, Massachusetts, Mississippi, and West Virginia, have filed suit against the tobacco industry.

■ POINTS TO CONSIDER

1. For the State of Minnesota, what is the basis of the case against tobacco?

2. What are Minnesota and BCBSM seeking from tobacco litigation?

3. Discuss how Minnesota claims this case differs from tobacco litigation in other states.

Excerpted from a State of Minnesota press release, "Questions & Answers Re: Tobacco Litigation," 1996.

*To this day, despite knowing that tobacco causes can-
cer and that nicotine is addictive, the tobacco companies continue to mislead the public, withhold what
they know and stifle development of safer cigarettes,
all while reaping billions of dollars in profits on their
deadly products.*

THE MAIN ALLEGATIONS

The lawsuit alleges that late in 1953, tobacco company execu-
tives met at the Plaza Hotel in New York and concocted a public
relations scheme to hide the truth about the hazards of smoking.
In January 1954, the tobacco companies ran advertisements in
newspapers throughout the country, including Minneapolis, St.
Paul, and Duluth, entitled "a frank statement to cigarette smokers." The tobacco industry promised in this advertisement and
other public statements that it would "promote the progress of
independent scientific research in the field of tobacco and health"
and cooperate "in efforts to learn and to make known all the
facts." In spite of these promises, the lawsuit alleges that the
industry has continued to deceive the public and conspires to suppress research and block development of a safer product.

The lawsuit charges that to this day, despite knowing that tobacco causes cancer and that nicotine is addictive, the tobacco companies continue to mislead the public, withhold what they know
and stifle development of safer cigarettes, all while reaping billions of dollars in profits on their deadly products. This landmark
case charges that the tobacco companies violated the public trust
through conspiracy, fraud and deception.

The suit is based on Minnesota's anti-trust and consumer protection laws. It charges that the tobacco industry promoted the
distribution and sale of products it knew to be harmful and con-
cealed research proving the addictive qualities of nicotine, while
conspiring to keep potentially safer products off the market. As a
result, the cost of health care has been inflated, penalizing purchasers such as the State of Minnesota and BCBSM (Blue Cross
Blue Shield of Minnesota).

WHAT ARE WE SEEKING?

Cigarettes kill six thousand Minnesotans every year – and cause
thousands more to contract cancer, heart disease, emphysema,

asthma and bronchitis. Cigarettes kill more people than the combined totals from alcohol, homicide, AIDS, cocaine, heroin and motor vehicles. Everyone in Minnesota is paying for this carnage – more than $350 million every year in health care costs in our state. (The precise portion of the $350 million paid by the State and by BCBSM is not yet determined.)

It's time for the tobacco companies to pay for the harm they have caused by their unlawful conspiracy and fraudulent conduct. Specifically, the State is seeking to recover the portion of the $350 million paid each year by the State to treat tobacco-related illnesses. BCBSM similarly is seeking to recover its damages caused by the tobacco industry. We also are seeking to put an end to the 40-year conspiracy and to force the tobacco companies to fund an independent, truthful campaign about smoking and to fund clinical smoking cessation programs in Minnesota to help remedy the harm they have caused.

DIFFERENT CASE

Our lawsuit is different in several significant ways.

(1) This is the first state lawsuit in the nation to allege an anti-trust conspiracy and consumer fraud against the tobacco companies;

(2) Previous lawsuits have challenged the tobacco companies mainly on the ground that their product is harmful, using product liability theories; this lawsuit says the tobacco companies should pay because of their conduct – an anti-trust and consumer fraud conspiracy that has caused great harm to the State and BCBSM;

(3) The State and BCBSM are joined together in this lawsuit – the two largest purchasers of health care services in Minnesota;

(4) In addition to seeking damages, we are seeking to force the tobacco companies to fund an independent public education campaign relating to the issues of smoking and health, to have the Council for Tobacco Research and the Tobacco Institute dissolved, and to have the tobacco companies fund clinical smoking cessation programs in the State of Minnesota to remedy their 40 years of conspiracy and fraud.

We are seeking to have the tobacco companies come clean with what they know to be the truth about smoking and pay for the damage to the State of Minnesota caused by their unlawful conduct. The tobacco companies are earning billions of dollars a year in profit. They can and should pay for the death and disease that they have caused in our State, and for the many millions of dollars that have been paid by Minnesota taxpayers – nonsmokers and smokers alike – for state-financed medical care for the victims of this conspiracy. But we can only remedy the harm done to Minnesotans. Congress, the FDA and other federal bodies will have to decide the industry's future.

In Minnesota, more than $350 million a year is spent to pay the health care expenses for disease caused by cigarettes. Of course, we are seeking much more than just the damages the State and BCBSM have suffered. In addition to damages, we're also seeking civil penalties, dissolution of the industry's research and propaganda apparatus, and seeking to force the tobacco companies to open their research files as they promised to do 40 years ago. They must tell the public everything they know about the harmful effects of cigarettes.

In this lawsuit we are seeking to recover damages that the State itself has incurred, which of course will be for the benefit of all of the taxpayers of Minnesota. It would not be practical in this case to represent individual smokers who have been harmed, for there are too many people with too many individual claims. BCBSM similarly is seeking to recover its damages for the benefit of its subscribers, who have paid increased premiums for health care coverage.

This case is unique, just as tobacco is unique. Unlike other products or activities that may harm one's health, cigarettes are the only consumer product that cause disease and death when used as the manufacturer intends. Moreover, we know of no other industry that has conspired like this to suppress research, defraud the public and prevent development of a safer product.

THE STATE AND BCBSM GOING FORWARD TOGETHER

The State and BCBSM are the two largest purchasers of health care services in the State. As such, they are perhaps the largest economic victims of the tobacco industry conspiracy in Minnesota. The lawsuit seeks recovery of the increased expenditures for health care services caused by the unlawful actions of the tobacco companies. Together, the State and BCBSM present the strongest possible front in going after the tobacco companies and seeking to recover for the damages they've caused.

This case is not about taxes.

(1) Paying taxes doesn't give anyone a license to engage in conspiracies or defraud the public. Corporations that violate the laws still must be accountable for the harm that they cause. For example, other companies that have produced harmful products, such as the Dalkon shield, have paid for the harm they have caused. That's all we're asking here – that the tobacco companies also pay for the damage that they have caused as a result of their unlawful conduct;

(2) Taxes don't come close to covering the harm caused by tobacco-related illnesses. Despite the massive health consequences of its product, the tobacco industry has never paid a cent in compensation to society. The basis of the suit is the illegal activity of the tobacco industry and the higher health care costs that have resulted from the industry's actions.

In some cases, smokers are charged higher premiums for insurance products, including some health coverage policies. However, most people receive health coverage through their employer. Group coverage does not lend itself to pricing products on an individual basis. In addition, it is not possible for an employer to monitor the behavior of employees and their families outside the workplace. Most importantly, however, the tobacco companies, not smokers, should pay for the damage caused by the tobacco companies' unlawful conduct.

PHILIP MORRIS DESTROYED DATA

Philip Morris, Inc. used an overseas laboratory to conduct some of its most critical smoking research and took steps to hide unfavorable results, including the destruction of documents, according to a memorandum compiled by the State of Minnesota in its lawsuit against the tobacco industry.

David Phelps, "Overseas Data Destroyed by Philip Morris," **Star Tribune** of Minneapolis, September 16, 1996.

ANTI-BUSINESS MESSAGE

This case is a statement of support for all the honest businesses of Minnesota. They don't conspire together to mislead the public. They don't conspire together, to stifle competition. They don't hold themselves above the law. In fact, to a large extent it's the honest businesses of Minnesota who are saddled unfairly with the added costs of health care that should be paid by the tobacco industry. Every business owner talks about the high cost of health care; anything we can do to lower the cost of health care will send a strong pro-business message. Our cases involve claims under Minnesota law for harm caused to the State by the tobacco companies. Of course, we would invite the federal government to pursue all appropriate actions against the tobacco companies as well.

READING

15

THE PICKPOCKET STATE

Jerry Taylor

Jerry Taylor is director of natural resource studies at the Cato Institute, a conservative, libertarian "think tank" in Washington, D.C. One of its primary concerns involves the relationship between the national economy and the role of government.

■ POINTS TO CONSIDER

1. According to the article, does tobacco consumption hurt the states monetarily? Why or why not?

2. How does the author criticize the states' logic in suing tobacco companies to recover Medicaid costs?

3. Discuss the implications of "socialized medicine" in light of the health issues surrounding tobacco consumption.

Jerry Taylor, "The Pickpocket State v. Tobacco," **Cato Institute**. April 20, 1996. Reprinted by permission.

Tobacco consumption is simply not a net burden on taxpayers.

Although the evidence is mounting that government can't do anything very well, it is undeniably true that there is one thing it remains quite good at: finding new and ingenious ways to pick the pockets of the American people.

POLITICIAN PICKPOCKETS

Like all good pickpockets, elected officials are adroit at identifying "marks," have an instinct for which pockets are most-heavily loaded with money, and are most successful when their victims are from the sociocultural "underworld."

And that's all you really need to know to understand why Florida, Massachusetts, Mississippi, Minnesota and West Virginia have filed suit against the tobacco industry to "recover" smoking-related Medicaid costs, and why the Liggett Group, the smallest of the major tobacco firms, has found its pockets now empty.

Of course, politicians don't advertise themselves as pickpockets; there's always some high-minded justification proffered for taking money that doesn't belong to them. In this particular case, they complain that states have been forced unfairly to foot the medical bills for those on Medicaid who smoke and that the tobacco industry, not the state taxpayer, should be paying the bills. Although it sounds fair enough, the complaint doesn't hold up to scrutiny.

TOBACCO CONTRIBUTION

First of all, tobacco consumption is simply not a net burden on taxpayers. The Florida suit, for example, alleges that the state spends $290 million annually on smoking-related illnesses. Yet in 1994, tobacco taxes added $1.9 billion to Florida's coffers, to say nothing of the $2.9 billion it contributed to state worker-compensation funds.

Nor is smoking a net burden on society as a whole. Economist W. Kip Viscusi of Duke University calculates that the total social cost of smoking-related disease, sick leave, fires, excess life insurance and foregone Social Security taxes amounts to $1.32 per pack. Yet, because smokers on average die earlier than nonsmokers, smokers save society $1.47 per pack in costs that otherwise might have been incurred for nursing homes, pension payments, Social Security benefits and other insurance costs. When one considers that smokers additionally pay tobacco taxes that average 53 cents per pack, one is hard-pressed to show that smokers are a net burden on anyone. If anything, society owes them money.

Second, the uncomfortable fact remains: if people don't die of smoking-related disease, they're going to die of something else. The states' lawsuits implicitly assume that if those Medicaid recipients didn't contract cancer or whatnot from smoking, they would not be imposing any costs on the state. Nonsense: they would contract heart disease, pneumonia, Alzheimer's disease, prostate cancer or any number of things. They would not live forever. The relevant question here is: do smokers impose greater burdens on Medicaid than nonsmokers? Given the staggering costs associated with extended nursing-home care and the cascading medical bills related to old age, I doubt it. Viscusi's data suggest, at best, a wash.

Third, the tobacco industry is not "forcing" state governments to cover the smoking-related medical bills of the poor; the federal government is. If states don't like footing those bills, their complaint is with Congress.

EXTREME LOGIC

Finally, the logic of the states' argument is pernicious in the extreme. One could just as easily argue that obesity-related diseases (300,000 deaths a year and $70 billion annually in medical costs) are a huge burden on state Medicaid programs and that snack food manufacturers ought to pony up. After all, their products have no nutritional value, are a leading cause of obesity, are disproportionately consumed by the poor and are highly addictive (Remember Lay's Potato Chips: "Bet you can't eat just one"?). Or what about meat consumption? According to a study last year in the peer-reviewed journal *Preventive Medicine*, meat is also a major cause of obesity and is directly responsible for $29 billion to $61 billion of the nation's medical costs.

THE MODERN TEMPERANCE MOVEMENT

Such arguments, of course, would be laughed out of the political arena, but that could change. A little more than a year ago, *The New York Times* published an op-ed from Kelly Brownell, director of the Yale Center for Eating and Weight Disorders, calling for a "fat tax" on snack foods and additional undefined steps to keep unhealthy food away from children. The point is, the argument for going after the snack-food industry (or, more immediately, the alcohol industry) to recover Medicaid costs is no different from the logic of going after the tobacco industry. One strikes us as absurd whereas the other does not. Why?

Unfortunately, the logic of socialized medicine leads us into this policy cul-de-sac. If we're all paying everyone else's medical bills, then each individual's eating habits, exercise regimen, recreational pursuits and social preferences ultimately become everyone's legitimate business. Of course, holding industry accountable for lifestyle decisions is more viable politically than going after everyone not living the life of a health fanatic, but the effect is the same.

The temperance movement of the 1920s demonstrated the futility of a direct assault on "sin." Our modern temperance movement realizes that bankrupting the peddlers of "sin" will accomplish through the back door what prohibition cannot accomplish through the front. A decent respect for a free society demands that we say no to both the pickpockets and the prohibitionists.

RECOVERING MEDICAID COSTS

The State of Florida

Governor Lawton M. Chiles, Jr., of Florida, along with the State of Florida Department of Business and Professional Regulation and the Agency for Health Care Administration (AHCA) filed a civil suit against various tobacco companies and tobacco interest in the 15th Circuit Court of Florida.

■ **POINTS TO CONSIDER**

1. Why is Florida suing the tobacco industry and tobacco interests?

2. Discuss the accusations made against the tobacco companies.

3. What authority does Florida have to pursue the tobacco manufacturers in court?

4. Does this action differ from the Minnesota lawsuit in previous readings? If so, explain.

Excerpted from the plaintiff brief filed in the Circuit Court of the Fifteenth Judicial Circuit in and for the County of Palm Beach, State of Florida, by the State of Florida.

The defendants have been able to privatize the profits while socializing the costs of their misconduct.

INTRODUCTION

Cigarette-related disease has killed and continues to kill untold millions of Americans. In the name of profits, cigarette manufacturers choose to ignore and suppress the truth about the hazards of cigarette smoking. As a result, Medicaid recipients have contracted smoking-related diseases including without limitation cancer, emphysema, and heart disease. The care of these Medicaid recipients has placed a significant burden on the State. This burden should rightfully be borne by the cigarette manufacturers. The Governor of the State of Florida has determined that the State of Florida can no longer afford to allow cigarette manufacturers to reap this windfall. Therefore, the Governor, the State of Florida and its various agencies as set out below have filed this lawsuit to force the cigarette manufacturers to pay for the health care crises their products have caused. The defendants have significantly benefited over many years from not having to pay the medical costs of the impoverished Medicaid recipients injured by their products and behavior. The defendants have been able to privatize the profits while socializing the costs of their misconduct. The impact on the State of Florida and its taxpayers has been felt in every department as the dollars flow out.

The Governor, the State of Florida, the Department of Business and Professional Regulation and the Agency for Health Care Administration do hereby bring this action pursuant to Florida Statute 409.910, et seq., as well as for the purposes of obtaining reimbursement for all money paid for medical assistance to Medicaid recipients as a result of diseases or injuries caused by the foreseeable and intended use of the defendants' tobacco products, cigarettes.

For many years, the State has incurred significant expenses associated with the provision of necessary health care and other such necessary assistance under the Medicaid programs to Medicaid recipients numbering in the thousands who suffer, or who have suffered, from tobacco-related injuries, diseases or sickness. This civil action is brought pursuant to Florida Statute 409.910, et seq., to obtain reimbursement of the State for the expenditures made to provide medical assistance to Medicaid recipients as a result of the actions of the defendants.

The defendants are a cartel who promote, market, distribute and sell cigarettes, and/or materially assist others in so doing to residents in Florida, and elsewhere throughout the United States, and have done so for many years. Under the Medicaid program, the State pays out large sums of money for the provision of necessary health care and other necessary assistance to eligible residents in Florida (Medicaid recipients), who have been and are now being treated in Palm Beach County, Florida, and elsewhere throughout the State, for tobacco-induced disease, injury and sickness, and the State has done so for many years. Thus, venue is proper in the Circuit Court of Palm Beach County, Florida.

At all pertinent times, the defendants purposefully and intentionally engaged in these activities, and continue to do so, knowing full well that when the State's residents used those cigarettes as they were intended to be used, that the State's residents would be substantially certain to suffer disease, injury and sickness, including cancer, emphysema, heart disease and other illnesses causing disability and death and that the State itself would be economically injured thereby.

Also at all pertinent times, the defendants purposefully and intentionally engaged in these activities, and continue to do so, knowing full well that the State would confer a benefit upon the defendants by providing or paying for health care and other necessary medical goods and services for certain of the State's residents thus harmed by the intended use of the defendants' cigarettes, and, in the absence of performance of such duty by the defendants, that the State itself thereby would be harmed.

Plaintiffs are not, at this time, making a claim for punitive damages but expect at the appropriate time to make a showing which supports an award of punitive damages and to thereafter amend their complaint pursuant to 768.72 of the Florida Statutes.

STATUTORY AUTHORITY

The Florida Legislature has authorized the Agency for Health Care Administration (AHCA) to initiate actions to recover the full amount of medical assistance provided by Medicaid. 409.910, Fla. Stat. The AHCA is authorized by Florida Statutes 409.910(9) to initiate or bring an action in order to recover in one proceeding all sums paid to provide medical assistance to all Medicaid recipients provided that (1) medical assistance has been provided to

Cartoon by Gary Markstein. Reprinted by permission.

more than one recipient; and (2) AHCA is seeking recovery from liable third parties due to the actions by the third parties or circumstances which involve common issues of fact or law.

The defendants herein are liable as third parties as a result of their participation in the manufacture, sale or distribution of cigarettes. These cigarettes are substantially interchangeable and a determination of the liability of each individual defendant involves the resolution of common issues of both fact and law. As a result, the State shall proceed under a market share theory.

CONDUCT ALLEGATIONS

The defendants listed above, and/or their predecessors and successors in interest, did business in the State of Florida; made contracts to be performed in whole or in part in Florida; and/or manufactured, tested, sold, offered for sale, supplied or placed in the stream of commerce, or, in the course of business, materially participated with others in so doing, cigarettes which the defendants knew to be defective, unreasonably dangerous and hazardous, and which the defendants knew would be substantially certain to cause injury to the State and to persons within Florida thereby negligently and intentionally causing injury to persons within Florida and to the State, and as described herein, committed and continue to commit tortuous and other unlawful acts in the State of Florida.

The State of Florida spends millions of dollars each year to provide or pay for health care and other necessary facilities and services on behalf of indigents and other eligible residents whose said health care costs are directly caused by tobacco-induced cardiovascular disease, lung cancer, emphysema, other respiratory diseases as well as the complications of pregnancy and childbirth including but not limited to low-weight babies.

The defendants have known for decades of the lethal dangers of smoking their cigarettes. By the late 1930's, based on published research, the tobacco companies had notice of the potential health hazards presented by smoking cigarettes. In 1946 tobacco company chemists themselves reported concern for the health of smokers. A 1953 report by Dr. Ernst L. Wynder heralded to the scientific community, and to the tobacco companies, a definitive link between cigarette smoking and cancer. In these tests, researchers painted condensed, puffed smoke onto the backs of mice. As a result thereof, the mice grew cancerous tumors. While previous statistical and epidemiologic studies had indicated a relationship between smoking and cancer, Dr. Wynder's study was the first conclusive biological study in this regard.

THE MANUFACTURE OF FRAUDULENT SCIENCE

In response to the publication of Dr. Wynder's study in 1953, the presidents of the leading tobacco manufacturers, including American Tobacco Co., R.J. Reynolds, Philip Morris, U.S. Tobacco Co., Lorillard, and Brown & Williamson Tobacco Corporation, hired the public relations firm of Hill and Knowlton,Inc., to deal with the "health scare" presented by smoking. Acting in concert, at a public relations strategy meeting, the participants decided to organize a committee to be specifically charged with the "public relations" function. This committee was engineered to take an offensive, pro-cigarettes stance despite the then obvious health dangers presented by cigarettes. As a result of these efforts, the Tobacco Institute Research Committee (TIRC), an entity later known as The Council for Tobacco Research (CTR), was formed.

110

FLORIDA SUPREME COURT

Florida's Supreme Court upheld most of a law that strips the tobacco industry of its best legal defenses and makes it easier for the state to sue for the costs of treating sick smokers.

"Florida Supreme Court Ruling," **Associated Press**, June 28, 1996.

The TIRC immediately ran a full-page promotion in more than 400 newspapers aimed at an estimated 43 million Americans. That piece was entitled "A Frank Statement to Cigarette Smokers." In this advertisement, the participating tobacco companies recognized their "special responsibility to the public," and promised to learn the facts about smoking and health. The participating tobacco companies promised to sponsor independent research on the subject, claiming they would make health a basic responsibility, paramount to any other consideration in their business. The participating tobacco companies also promised to cooperate closely with public health officials. However, these promises so publicly and dramatically made to the public, the residents of the State of Florida and government regulators were breached over and over again.

The strategy employed by the tobacco companies and aided and abetted by the Tobacco Trade Associations was a strategy best described as see no evil, hear no evil, and speak no evil concerning the health effects of cigarette smoking.

READING

17

STATE LITIGATION THREATENS MORE THAN TOBACCO

Samuel Francis

Samuel Francis is a nationally syndicated columnist. He wrote the following article for Tribune Media Services.

■ POINTS TO CONSIDER

1. According to Francis, what do these lawsuits do to the concept of personal responsibility?

2. Discuss why the idea of "extended liability" is far reaching beyond the tobacco companies, according to the author.

3. Describe the "English rule," and the effect it will have on litigation.

4. Why does the author accuse "Big Tobacco" of being the "Big Chicken?"

*The liability laws play to all the collectivist mytholo-
gies of our age, presupposing that it is not the individual user of tobacco who is at fault.*

What gun control was to the political gestapoids last year,
smoke control is this year. In Maryland, liberal Gov. Parris
Glendenning has just banned smoking in all private workplaces, a
decree that could bankrupt small bars and restaurants as their
puffing customers go home – or across state lines – to puff in private.

No one was permitted to vote on the measure, and the governor's *diktat* reconfirmed an earlier rule last year that issued from
the bowels of the state bureaucracy. Maryland state legislators are
now modifying the governor's blatantly undemocratic act, but in
other states also, the war on smoking and smokers is escalating.

THE LATEST TACTIC

The latest tactic is to try to hold tobacco companies liable for
health care costs that accrue to the state because of smoking-related diseases. Since the Smoke Nazis don't hesitate to invent
phony evidence that "relate" smoking to every illness except
ingrown toenails, the transparent goal of the new liability laws is
to bankrupt the companies and thereby effectively outlaw the
manufacture and sale of tobacco.

Florida is the latest (and fourth) state to try the liability trick, and
Gov. Lawton Chiles, does not hesitate to play the demagogue in
blaming "Big Tobacco" for "ruining" the lives of the folk who buy
and use its products. The other states are Minnesota,
Massachusetts and – of all places – Mississippi, which has the
dubious distinction of possessing an attorney general who might
be a happier soul if he lived in the peoples' republics to the far
north.

The liability laws play to all the collectivist mythologies of our
age, presupposing that (a) it is not the individual user of tobacco
who is at fault but the folks who somehow "coerced" him into
using it, and (b) it's not the state, which has chosen to assume the
burden of paying for health care, that should pay for these particular health costs but (again) those "responsible" for causing the diseases.

The reality is that under this concept of legal liability, the whole notion of responsibility goes up in – well – smoke. It ignores the plain fact that tobacco patrons choose to puff and are almost universally aware of the health dangers linked to smoking and that, therefore, responsibility for getting sick because of smoking lies at the door of those who do it.

EXTENDED LIABILITY

Under the extended liability concept, there is virtually no product or service that would be safe from litigation. If you slice off your nose one morning while shaving, you or your heirs could sue the razor companies. If you drop your electric toothbrush in the swimming pool and fricassee the neighborhood kids over for a dip, their families could sue not only you but also the toothbrush company, the swimming pool maker and maybe even the water company for not inventing non-conductive water. The new liability is just a bit more than a threat to Big Tobacco; it threatens the whole economic, legal and even moral fabric.

DETER LITIGATION

The tobacco companies are grousing about the spread of the concept, but so far they don't seem to know how to fight it. One man who does know is Mike Gunn, a young state senator in Mississippi who has come up with a simple proposal to deter his state's ill-advised plan to sue the companies for state health cost.

Mr. Gunn's solution is called the "English rule" (exactly why I can't tell you), but under it, whenever the state sues anyone and loses in court, the state has to pick up the entire tab for the court costs. Thus, attorney generals who might be happier wrecking the laws and morals of places like Massachusetts rather than those of more civilized places like Mississippi would have to think twice before they sally into court and bray about the evil tobacco companies (or any other company that happens to be the fashionable monster of the hour).

But no matter how "evil" you might think the tobacco companies are, they're mainly just stupid. They did virtually nothing to support Mr. Gunn's proposal, and though it passed the state senate, the Smoke Nazis gutted it in the house. Terrified of controversy and confrontation, "Big Tobacco," like much of big business, is mainly a Big Chicken when it comes to defending itself and the basic liberties the Smoke Nazis seek to destroy.

Lots of people dislike smoking, but what its enemies are now pushing goes well beyond its health hazards and strikes at the heart and lungs of moral and legal responsibility. Lots of other Americans, smokers or not, are waking up to the danger they pose, but their fight would be easier if the companies that sell tobacco would stand up for their own interests, if not for anyone else's.

INTERPRETING EDITORIAL CARTOONS

This activity may be used as an individualized study guide for students in libraries and resource centers or as a discussion catalyst in small group and classroom discussions.

Although cartoons are usually humorous, the main intent of most political cartoonists is not to entertain. Cartoons express serious social comment about important issues. Using graphic and visual arts, the cartoonist expresses opinions and attitudes. By employing an entertaining and often light-hearted visual format, cartoonists may have as much or more impact on national and world issues as editorial and syndicated columnists.

Points to Consider:

1. Examine the cartoon on page 117.

2. How would you describe the message of the cartoon? Try to describe the message in one to three sentences.

3. Do you agree with the message expressed in the cartoon? Why or why not?

4. Does the cartoon support the author's point of view in any of the readings in this publication? If the answer is yes, be specific about which reading or readings and why.

5. Are any of the readings in Chapter Four in basic agreement with the cartoon?

CHAPTER 5

ECONOMICS, EXPORTS AND ETHICS

READING

18

TOBACCO PRICE SUPPORT: AN OVERVIEW OF THE PROGRAM

Jasper Womach

Jasper Womach is a specialist in agricultural policy. He prepared the following report for the Congressional Research Service (CRS) where he works in the Environment and Natural Resources Policy Division. CRS Reports are prepared for members and committees of Congress.

■ POINTS TO CONSIDER

1. Summarize the size and economy of tobacco farming in the U.S. and worldwide.

2. Discuss the reasons why tobacco price support was established.

3. How does the program function?

4. What effect did passage of the "No Net Cost Tobacco Program Act" have for the federal government?

Womach, Jasper, Tobacco Price Support: An Overview of the Program, **CRS**, Washington, D.C.: 16 Mar. 1994.

The federal tobacco price support program limits and stabilizes the quantity of tobacco produced and marketed by farmers.

SUMMARY

Over 94 percent of U.S. tobacco production is flue-cured and burley (both being cigarette tobacco types). These crops are particularly important to the agriculture of North Carolina (where flue-cured is grown) and Kentucky (where burley is grown). Together, these states produce 65 percent of the total U.S. tobacco crop. The federal tobacco price support program is designed to support and stabilize prices for farmers. It operates through a combination of mandatory marketing quotas and loans. Marketing quotas limit the amount of tobacco each farmer can sell, which indirectly raises market prices. The loan program establishes guaranteed minimum prices. The law requires that the loan program operate at no net cost to the federal government. In several recent years, the tobacco program has actually shown net revenues in the federal budget because old loan repayments have exceeded new loan outlays. Apart from year-to-year budget impacts, no-net-cost provisions of the program assure that all loan principal plus interest will be recovered.

INDUSTRY PROFILE

World production of tobacco is estimated at about 18.9 billion pounds for 1993. Though data are collected for 107 countries, about 75 percent of world tobacco is produced in the following ten countries: China (8,106 mil. lbs.), United States (1,605 mil. lbs.), Brazil (1,340 mil. lbs.), India (1,272 mil. lbs.), Turkey (659 mil. lbs.), Zimbabwe (518 mil. lbs.), Indonesia (337 mil. lbs.), Italy (328 mil. lbs.), Greece (328 mil. lbs.), and Malawi (300 mil. lbs.).

Some 115,000 U.S. farms grew about 1,605 million pounds of tobacco on about 745,000 acres in 1993. The estimated farm value of the1993 crop is $2.8 billion. Major U.S. tobaccos are flue-cured (produced primarily in North Carolina) and burley (produced primarily in Kentucky), which are both cigarette tobaccos. Other types of tobacco are used for cigars, chewing, and snuff.

Tobacco is grown in 16 states. However, North Carolina and Kentucky originate 65 percent of total production. Four other States (Tennessee, Virginia, South Carolina, and Georgia) produce

120

another 26 percent. The high per acre value of tobacco (averaging $3,758 in 1993) makes it critical to the income of the growers and important to the economies of the major producing states. For North Carolina in 1993, tobacco constituted 20 percent of the value of all farm commodities (crops and livestock) and 44 percent of all crop production; for Kentucky, tobacco accounted for 27 percent of the value of all commodities and 55 percent of crop production.

The United States is the world's largest exporter of manufactured tobacco products and about equal to Brazil as a top exporter of unmanufactured tobacco leaf. During 1993, the United States exported 458 million pounds (farm weight) of leaf tobacco, valued at $1.31 billion. Major foreign leaf markets were Germany, Japan, and the Netherlands. The value of manufactured tobacco product exports was $4.25 billion. The largest export cigarette markets were Japan, Belgium-Luxembourg, Hong Kong, Saudi Arabia, and United Arab Emirates.

THE PRICE SUPPORT PROGRAM

The tobacco price support program exists only for the economic benefit of farmers. It was created for the purpose of supporting the income and stabilizing the price of tobacco received by farmers. The choice of whether or not federal support will be provided is determined by growers in a referendum held every three years.

When producers approve federal price support for tobacco, they become subject to marketing quotas. Marketing quotas are a supply control mechanism that indirectly increases market prices. At the same time, the federal government is required to guarantee prices at least as high as the level specified in the law.

MARKETING QUOTAS

When farmers vote in favor of price supports, they are at the same time agreeing to accept government restrictions on the amount of tobacco they can market. The national marketing quota is the amount judged sufficient to meet domestic and export demand, but at a price above the government support price. Each farm's quota is assigned to the land. So, the right to produce and market a specified quantity of tobacco resides with the owner of the land. A farmer can only begin to grow tobacco by purchasing or renting land that has a quota. By limiting the supply of tobacco, the market price is increased. Total farm revenue is raised because consumption does not decline enough to offset the price increase. In this way, farm income is supposed to be supported through artificially high market prices, rather than through direct government payments. This differs from other commodity price support programs that utilize direct payments as the principal support mechanism rather than marketing quotas.

LOANS

Marketing quotas are not always totally effective at supporting market prices given the numerous variables that affect tobacco supply and demand. Consequently, federal support prices are guaranteed through the mechanism of non-recourse loans available on each farmer's marketed crop. The loan price for each type of tobacco is announced each year by the Secretary of Agriculture, who uses the formula specified in the law to calculate loan levels. The national loan price on 1993 crop flue-cured tobacco was $1.577 per pound; the burley loan price was $1.683.

At the auction sale barn, each lot of tobacco goes to the highest bidder, unless that bid does not exceed the government's loan price. In such cases, the farmer is paid the loan price by a cooperative, with money borrowed from the CCC. The tobacco is consigned to the cooperative (known as a price stabilization cooperative), which redries, packs, and stores the tobacco as collateral for CCC. The cooperative, acting as an agent for the CCC, later sells the tobacco, with the proceeds going to repay the loan from CCC.

NO-NET-COST AND MARKETING ASSESSMENTS

Under the threat of legislative dissolution of the program by its opponents, Congress passed the No-Net-Cost Tobacco Program Act in 1982. This legislation imposes an assessment on every pound of tobacco marketed. The no-net-cost assessment on 1993 crop flue-cured was 2.423 cents per pound; the burley assessment was 2.817 cents per pound. Growers and buyers each pay a portion of the no-net-cost assessment. Beginning in 1994, imported tobacco is subject to the no-net-cost assessment. The assessment funds (amounting to about $40 million in 1993) are deposited in an escrow account that is held to reimburse the government for any financial losses resulting from tobacco loan operations.

READING

19

CONTINUING THE TOBACCO PROGRAM SENDS MIXED MESSAGES

Richard D. Lueker and the Coalition on Smoking OR Health

Richard D. Lueker, M.D. is a practicing cardiologist in Albuquerque, New Mexico, and is affiliated with Presbyterian Hospital Center, New Heart Rehabilitation and the University of New Mexico. The Coalition on Smoking OR Health, based in Washington, D.C., is an umbrella group for the American Cancer Society, the American Heart Association, and the American Lung Association. The Coalition works to inform public policy makers about tobacco and disease prevention and to promote policy initiatives designed to reduce tobacco use.

■ POINTS TO CONSIDER

1. What mixed message is the government sending with the tobacco program?

2. How have small tobacco farmers suffered, according to the author, in the past 30 years?

3. According to the article, summarize tobacco farmers' attitudes toward diversification.

Excerpted from the statement of Richard D. Lueker, M.D. before the Subcommittee on Agriculture, Rural Development and Related Agencies of the House of Representatives Appropriations Committee, April 18, 1996 and excerpted from a position paper, "Federal Support for Tobacco" released by the Coalition on Smoking OR Health. Reproduced with permission. © American Heart Association, World Wide Web, Heart and Stroke Guide, 1996. Copyright 1996.

Tobacco, a highly addictive drug, is responsible for over 400,000 deaths each year in the U.S. On the other hand, policies of the USDA assure that federal assistance and tax dollars support the growth and use of tobacco products.

Richard D. Lueker Statement:

I wish to address two issues, U.S. policies in support of the growth of tobacco and the proposed initiative by the Food and Drug Administration to reduce youth access to tobacco. As we have done on a number of past occasions, the Coalition on Smoking OR Health would like to address the tobacco-related expenditures of the United States Department of Agriculture (USDA).

TAXPAYER COSTS

Although the tobacco support program is called a "No-Net-Cost" program, the U.S. taxpayers still finance $16 million annually to administer the program and appropriate $27 million for additional tobacco-related expenses such as extension services, forecasting, agricultural statistics, world market analysis, inspection and grading and crop insurance. These tobacco-related expenditures would be significantly higher if not for the cuts made during the appropriations cycles. As recently as FY 1993, $8 million dollars was spent on tobacco-related research. Much of this research was aimed at enhancing the production and marketing of tobacco.

MIXED MESSAGES

These expenditures continue to send a mixed message to the American taxpayer. Tobacco, a highly addictive drug, is responsible for over 400,000 deaths each year in the U.S. On the other hand, policies of the USDA assure that federal assistance and tax dollars support the growth and use of tobacco products. U.S. policy should not continue policies and programs that encourage and promote the growth of tobacco. The cost of administering the program and related activities should be borne by the industry which benefits from its programs. We do, however, strongly believe that the nation's tobacco farmers have been mistreated by the U.S. tobacco industry. While the tobacco farmers' share of the value of tobacco products has plummeted from 16 percent of every dollar's worth of tobacco products sold in 1957 to a mere 3 percent in 1991, the tobacco industry's share has increased to over 60 percent.

In 1969, U.S. manufactured cigarettes contained 90 percent American-grown tobacco. By the 1990s, that figure had dropped to barely 60 percent. While American tobacco companies continue to expand their overseas manufacturing and growing investments, tobacco manufacturing jobs in the U.S. fell from 1982-92 by 19,600 jobs, a 29 percent decline. Over a similar period, the total number of tobacco farms fell by 42,000, a 23 percent decline. Federal funds would be better spent facilitating the growth of alternative crops and improving access to markets for other crops than helping to support the growth of tobacco in a declining market.

DIVERSIFICATION

A November 1995 study released by the Center for Sustainable Systems and the Bowman Gray School of Medicine at Wake Forest University reveals tobacco farmers' attitudes toward diversifying their farms and lessening their financial dependence on tobacco. Their U.S. Tobacco Farmers' Opinion Study was conducted among a geographically and economically diverse group of growers. Among their findings:

- 67% of tobacco farmers under 45 years of age were "interested" or "very interested" in trying other on-farm ventures to supplement or replace tobacco.

- 72% cited a lack of processing facilities for other crops as a barrier to diversification, 60% cited lack of capital, and 57% thought low-interest loans would be needed.

The group also polled the general public regarding tobacco farming:

- 75% believed the U.S. government should not subsidize tobacco farmers.

- 57% favored tax money going to programs to help tobacco farmers diversify.

- 66% believed the government should actively help farmers find other ways to make a living.

REDEFINING POLICY

Let's redefine U.S. policy towards tobacco. Recently, the House fell just a few votes shy of passing Mr. Durbin's floor amendment to the Agriculture Appropriations measure which would have restricted taxpayer funds for tobacco-related expenditures in the USDA. The Coalition on Smoking OR Health urges support for a similar amendment, in addition to passing on the administrative costs to the tobacco industry.

Coalition on Smoking OR Health Statement:

The American Heart Association and the Coalition on Smoking OR Health support efforts to eliminate federal financial support for the growth of tobacco while assisting farmers who wish to stop growing tobacco. Possible mechanisms include:

- Eliminating the use of federal funds to administer or otherwise support the tobacco-related programs. Currently the U.S. Department of Agriculture spends over $16 million annually to administer the federal tobacco support program ("No-Net-Cost Tobacco Program") in addition to approximately $27 million for other tobacco-related activities.

- Creating a federally funded program using revenues from increasing federal tobacco taxes for:

- Providing assistance to farmers in converting from tobacco to other crops and improving access of such farmers to markets for other crops

- Providing grants or loans to communities and persons involved in the production or manufacture of tobacco or tobacco products to support economic diversification plans that provide economic alternatives to tobacco for such communities or persons

- Providing funds for government purchase of tobacco allotments for purposes of retiring such allotments for farmers who choose to terminate their growth of tobacco.

BACKGROUND

From its inception in 1982, the Coalition on Smoking OR Health has opposed the inconsistency of the federal government's policies on tobacco. The policies acknowledge that cigarette

ELIMINATE SUPPORT PROGRAMS

As agreed, we have reviewed issues associated with the advertisement and promotion of U.S. cigarettes in Japan, Taiwan, South Korea, Thailand, Hong Kong, Malaysia, and Indonesia. This report provides information on (1) the continuation of the conflicting U.S. government policies of pursuing anti-smoking initiatives domestically while assisting U.S. cigarette companies in selling their products abroad.

General Accounting Office Report on federal support for U.S. Tobacco Company advertising efforts in foreign countries, December 3, 1992.

smoking is the single most preventable cause of death in the United States while allocating federal funds for scientific research and public education about the health hazards of smoking. But other government policies provide federal assistance and tax dollars to support the growth of tobacco.

The coalition is concerned about the economic welfare of the tobacco farmer. The coalition understands the need for Congress and the public to consider the welfare of the tobacco farmer as Congress debates how to best eliminate the government's role in the tobacco price-support program. The issue is not whether federal financial support for the tobacco support program should be ended, but how quickly and fairly this can be accomplished.

READING

20

DRIVING TOBACCO FARMERS OUT OF BUSINESS IS NOT THE ANSWER

Wendell Berry

Wendell Berry is a Kentucky poet, tobacco farmer, and non-smoker.

■ POINTS TO CONSIDER

1. What community and environmental benefits of tobacco cultivation does Berry discuss?

2. How has tobacco growing become part of an "authentic moral issue?"

3. In his tobacco dialogue, what points does Berry make? Discuss the validity of his points.

4. Analyze the consequences of eliminating the tobacco program, according to Berry.

Wendell Berry, "Our Tobacco Problem," **The Progressive**, May 1992. Reprinted by permission from **The Progressive**, 409 East Main Street, Madison, WI 53703.

We ought to be aware of our inconsistency in condemning tobacco and excusing other damaging addictions, some of which are much more threatening than tobacco.

To many people nowadays, there is nothing complex about the moral issue of tobacco. They are, simply, against it. They will sit in their large automobiles, spewing a miasma of toxic gas into the atmosphere, and they will thank you for not smoking a cigarette. They will sit in a smoke-free bar, drinking stingers and other lethal beverages, and wonder how smokers can have so little respect for their bodies. They will complacently stand in the presence of a coal-fired power plant or a nuclear power plant or a bomb factory or a leaking chemical plant, and they will wonder how a tobacco farmer could have so little regard for public health.

Well, as always, it matters whose ox is being gored. And tobacco, I am obliged to confess, is my ox.

A TOBACCO COMMUNITY

I was born in the tobacco country of Kentucky, into a family preoccupied with the cultivation, the economy, and the politics of tobacco. Many of my closest and dearest friends have been, and are, tobacco growers. I have worked in the crop from early childhood until now. I have liked and often enjoyed the work. I love the crop in all of its stages. I think tobacco is a beautiful plant. I love the lore and the conversation of tobacco growing. I love the smell of tobacco and of tobacco smoke.

Burley tobacco (a thin-bodied, air-cured tobacco), as I first knew it, was produced with an intensity of care and a refinement of skill that far exceeded that given to any food crop that I know about. It was a handmade crop; between plant bed and warehouse, every plant, every leaf, was looked at, touched, appraised, lifted, and carried many times. The experience of growing up in a community in which virtually everybody was passionately interested in the quality of a local product was, I now see, a rare privilege.

It is hardly too much to say that we were a tobacco culture. It was our staple crop, the cornerstone of our economy. Because of "the program," which limited production in order to control price, the tobacco market was the only market on which the farmer was

129

dependably not a victim. Though we practiced a diversified way of farming, our farming focused on tobacco. The rhythm of our farming year, as of our financial year, was set by the annual drama of the tobacco crop. Because so much handwork was involved in the growing of tobacco, it was also a sociable crop, with much cooperation among farmers.

There is another, more practical benefit of tobacco that must be mentioned. For a sloping, easily eroded countryside such as I live in, and such as makes up much of the "tobacco belt," tobacco has been an ideal crop, simply because it has permitted significant income to be realized from small acreages, thereby sparing us the inevitable damage of extensive plowing, and because it has fit well with the pattern of livestock farming.

A MORAL ISSUE

I have said as much good of it as I know. But of course everything to be said about tobacco is not good. Although there have always been people who disliked it, tobacco has become an authentic moral issue only within the past 30 years, and for two reasons: The case against it as a threat to health became extremely persuasive; and, in spite of this widely recognized threat, tobacco continues to be grown, and tobacco products continue to be advertised and sold. There is, in my opinion, no way to deny that this is a most serious moral predicament, and no way to evade the questions raised by it.

TOBACCO CONVERSATIONS

Because I have written a good bit about farmers who raise tobacco, and because I have spoken in defense of the federal tobacco farming program, I often fall into conversations on the subject with people who are indignant. These conversations are always fragmentary, because of the great complexity of the subject, and I have never been satisfied with any of them. And so I would like, now, to attempt something like a complete dialogue:

"Do you smoke?" I am asked. And I reply, "No." **"Did you ever smoke?"** "Yes, from the age of 14 until I was 30." **"Why did you quit?"** "Two reasons. One, I had young children." **"So you do agree that smoking tobacco is unhealthy!"** "Yes, though I still have some questions on the subject. Since, for example, there is nobody today whose lungs are polluted only with tobacco smoke,

I SAY WE LET
CLINTON DECLARE
TOBACCO A DRUG...
THAT WAY, HE'LL
LEAVE US ALONE!

CULPEPER'S
TOBACCO
FARM WHOLESALE RETAIL

Cartoon by Richard Wright. Reprinted by permission.

I would like to know what contribution other pollutants may make
to 'tobacco-caused' diseases. And since very few people now
smoke chemical-free tobacco, I would like to know the effect of
the residues of agricultural chemicals in the tobacco. But, yes, I
do believe that smoke inhalation is unhealthy. Firefighters can
testify to this, as can most citizens of industrial societies." **"But
most modern smoke is inhaled unwillingly. Why would anyone
willingly inhale smoke that is dangerous to health?"** "Well, to
start with, sociability." **"Sociability?"** "Tobacco smoke is fra-
grant, and smoking at its best is convivial or ceremonious and
pleasant. Some would say it is a comfort. But you haven't asked
me my second reason for quitting." **"What is your second reason?"** "Addiction. I didn't like being addicted. I had got so I
could smoke a cigarette without even knowing it. There was no
pleasure in that." **"You're against addiction, then?"** "I'm against
addiction to all things that are damaging and unnecessary. We
are an addictive society, rushing from one expensive and dangerous fix to another." **"But say we are an addictive society, does
that make the tobacco addiction right or excusable?"** "Of course
not. It only means we ought to be aware of our inconsistency in
condemning tobacco and excusing other damaging addictions,

131

some of which are much more threatening than tobacco." **"But the question remains, how can you have quit smoking yourself, because you recognize the danger, and yet support the tobacco economy?"** "I don't support the tobacco economy, which involves much – seductive advertising, for one thing – that I don't like. I support the tobacco program." **"What is that?"**

THE TOBACCO PROGRAM

"To risk oversimplification, it is an arrangement, sponsored by the federal government, approved by the farmers in a specially held vote, by which they agree to limit production in order to secure a livable return on investment and labor. This strategy of production control is commonplace in other productive industries, rare in farming. But the tobacco program has worked well. In my part of the country, it has assured the survival of thousands of small farmers for more than half a century." **"Why should these people receive a government subsidy for growing a crop that the government acknowledges to be dangerous?"** "It is not a subsidy. The tobacco that falls below the support price is placed under loan by the program, the title to the crop remaining with the farmer until its sale at a later date. The government supplies the loan, which is repaid with interest and all expenses. And for several years, tobacco farmers and manufacturers have been assessed one cent each per pound to pay administrative and other costs, so that the program can be operated at no net cost to taxpayers." **"But it's tobacco they're growing. To support the program is to support tobacco and everything that goes with it."** "Well, let me ask you a question. Do you think people are going to quit smoking?" **"I suppose, considering the failure of Prohibition and the current popularity of illegal drugs, the answer is probably no."** "And if some people continue to use it, other people will continue to grow it – is that not right?" **"I suppose it is."** "And so, if you destroyed the program, destroying in the process the farmers who depend on the program, who would grow the tobacco?" **"I haven't thought much about that. Large corporate growers under contract to the tobacco companies? Cheap laborers in Third World countries? I don't know."** "Most of the farmers who now grow it would, at any rate, be out of business, and the loss of the program would be extremely painful, disorienting, and costly for many thousands of families. So, you see, to support the program is only to say that, if tobacco is to be grown, you want it to be grown by the people who have always grown it – not by the sort for whom the failure of these people would be a 'window of opportunity.' You see, tobacco farmers have no alternative at present to growing tobacco, none at all. That's why their 'choice' to grow tobacco is really not a choice. They have had, as farmers, nothing else to choose." **"What sort of alternative do they need?"** "They need a crop, or several crops, that can produce a comparable income from comparable acreages, that can be grown with family and neighborhood labor, and for which there is a dependable market." **"They need to be growing food crops, you mean – fruits and vegetables."** "I think so. Along with the meat and milk that they already produce." **"I see you are still clinging to the idea of an agricultural economy of diversified small farms producing for local markets and local consumers."** "Yes, I'm still clinging to it. I want people to continue to eat. I want them to have, as dependably as possible, a local supply of good food. I want their food budget to support a thriving population of local farmers. That way, the land will thrive."

"And you see the tobacco farmers as necessary to that?"

"I see all farmers – all that are left, and, I hope, some more – as necessary to that. Tobacco farmers are farmers, and among the best of farmers; their 'know-how' is a great public asset, if the public only knew it. They are farming some very good land. They should be growing food for the people of their region, the people of neighboring cities – or they should have a viable choice of doing so. The people who so eagerly condemn them for growing tobacco should be just as eager to help them to find alternative crops. Tobacco growing is a problem to be solved, but so far state government and the universities show little interest in solving it. The difficulties are enormous, and they had better be acknowledged. For one thing, the idea of local food economies, or 'local food self-sufficiency,' has few advocates and, so far as I know, no powerful ones; it has been eclipsed by the 'global economy' and the 'free market.' For another, most people are satisfied, so far, with the present system of food supply – though it is a satisfaction based upon ignorance. And, most difficult of all, if we are to wean farmers from tobacco onto other crops, we must somehow cause a local demand and a local supply to come into existence simultaneously."

"Do you foresee no help with this from the federal government?"

"The federal government's agricultural policy has been to leave

133

the markets unregulated and production uncontrolled, and let the farmers compete against each other year after year to survive the overproduction that is the result of their competition. We need to make it possible for farmers to choose not to grow tobacco and continue farming, and we need a better, safer, fresher supply of food, which is to say a local supply. And these two needs are, in fact, the same, for the more local the more fresh. And as you shorten the distance between consumer and producer, you increase the consumer's power to know and influence the quality of food. Kentucky consumers, for instance, could influence Kentucky farmers much more easily than they could influence California farmers. Moreover, 'fresh' implies short distances, and therefore lower expenditures for transportation, packaging, refrigeration, and national advertising campaigns. A local food economy, in short, implies higher prices for farmers and lower costs to consumers. Individuals and groups could start buying produce from local farmers. The government's approval is not necessary. In fact, the process has already begun. Scattered all over the country there are farmers who are selling produce directly to urban consumers. Local merchants sometimes stock local produce. If churches and conservation organizations – the two groups with most reason to be concerned – would get involved, much more could be accomplished. That is the way it will grow."

"Are you talking about some kind of revolution?"

"I'm talking about economic secession – just quietly forming the means of withdrawal, not from the tobacco economy alone, but from the entire economy of exploitive land use that is ruining both the countryside and the country communities. Its principle would simply be good use – the possibility, often demonstrated, that land and people can be used without destroying them. It would understand, first of all, that the ruin of farmers solves no problem, and makes many."

READING **21**

THE EXPORT OF TOBACCO IS HARD TO DEFEND

Peter G. Bourne and the
National Catholic Reporter

Peter G. Bourne wrote the following comments in his capacity as president of the American Association for World Health. The National Catholic Reporter (NCR) *is an independent Catholic newsweekly based in Kansas City, Missouri.*

■ **POINTS TO CONSIDER**

1. Summarize the global health problems that tobacco use causes.

2. Contrast American policy on illicit drug traffic and legal tobacco export. Does Bourne adequately reveal hypocrisy?

3. Discuss the "irony" in tobacco export to Vietnam.

Peter Bourne, "An Evil the United States Shouldn't Send Overseas," **Los Angeles Times**, May 1989. Reprinted by permission of Peter G. Bourne. "Tobacco Firms Out to Spread Woe Worldwide," **National Catholic Reporter**, 16 Feb. 1996: 40. Reprinted by permission, **National Catholic Reporter**, Kansas City, Missouri. Subscriptions: 1-800-333-7373.

PETER G. BOURNE

The traditional rationale given for this country's campaign against drug abuse is the need to protect the health of America's youth. Increasingly on this basis we have been willing to accept that tobacco needs to be included in the same category as other drugs of abuse.

A primary element of the anti-drug campaign of all recent administrations, and especially the Reagan and Bush administrations, has been to gain the collaboration of the governments of drug-producing countries in preventing the trafficking of drugs to the United States. But at the same time, our government has actively promoted the sale of U.S. tobacco products to the rest of the world.

An estimated 10,000 individuals die worldwide each year from the effect of illicit drugs. More than 2.5 million die from the effects of tobacco. More Colombians die from the effects of American tobacco than do Americans from cocaine, and more Thais die from our tobacco than do Americans from Southeast Asian heroin.

As if this were not bad enough, the office of the U.S. trade representative has threatened three countries with trade sanctions for refusing to open up their markets to United States tobacco products, and is threatening other countries that have banned or are strictly regulating their advertisement and promotion.

The United States cannot plausibly lead the global effort to control drug trafficking while it remains the world's primary purveyor of drug-related death and disease through the export of its tobacco products. Nor will the argument that heroin and cocaine use must be curbed at all cost because of the health threat they pose to our youth have much credibility in the rest of the world.

The inevitable conclusion is that our drug policies are fundamentally determined not primarily by health concerns but by economic interests. As a rich and powerful nation, we are determined to define as legal a drug we can export at immense profit to the rest of the world, regardless of the health consequences – while denying largely impoverished countries access to the lucrative U.S. market because they cultivate drugs we have defined as illegal.

Cartoon by Steve Kelly. Reprinted by permission of **Copley News Service.**

The Bush administration had a unique opportunity to establish clearly that health considerations are the basis for our anti-drug policy. No clearer signal could be sent than to state unequivocally that the U.S. government will do nothing to help promote the sale of tobacco products overseas, much less inflict sanctions against nations that seek to curtail their use. Such a statement would go far to reestablish the sagging credibility of the President's anti-drug effort and provide strong leadership for the war on drugs worldwide.

NATIONAL CATHOLIC REPORTER

It is widely known that cigarettes lead to the deaths of some 500,000 people in the United States each year. According to estimates, tobacco use overseas, now rising quickly, kills another 2.5 million people worldwide each year.

Health officials estimate that worldwide tobacco use causes about 90 percent of lung cancer deaths, 30 percent of all cancers, 20-25 percent of coronary heart diseases and stroke deaths and more than 80 percent of chronic bronchitis and emphysema.

WORLD TOBACCO USE

Although tobacco companies are on the defensive in the United States and Canada, they are clearly winning the battle for the hearts and lungs of many of the world's people. The World Health Organization reports that 1.1 billion people worldwide smoke, including nearly half of all males...

China alone has 350 million smokers, more than the entire population of the United States. About 3 million Chinese begin puffing every year...

The prime markets are Latin America, Africa, Southeast Asia, China, the former Soviet Union and Eastern Europe – the world's most populous regions...

Sonni Efron, "World Still Lighting Up," **Los Angeles Times**, September 14, 1996.

With pressure gradually growing to curtail cigarette smoking in the United States, the tobacco companies, including the Philip Morris Co., The British American Tobacco Co., Rothmans International Co. and R.J. Reynolds Tobacco Co., – with the help of U.S. government officials – have been developing new markets for tobacco export. They are targeting Asia in particular.

In the late 1980s, Japan, Korea and Taiwan were all forced to repeal restrictions on cigarette advertising under U.S. trade threats. Concurrently, total consumption of cigarettes in those nations increased from 410 billion in 1986 to 455 billion in 1989.

In Japan, cigarette ads rose from 40th to second place in total television air-time in one year following the entry of U.S. companies; two-thirds of the ads were for U.S. brands. The combined 1988 advertising budgets of three U.S. tobacco companies in South Korea made U.S. cigarettes one of the country's most heavily advertised products.

Young Asians in particular have been picking up the deadly habit: A 1988 Japanese survey found that 25 percent of female high school seniors smoked compared to 13 percent of adult women. The smoking rate among Taiwanese high school students jumped from 22 percent the year before U.S. companies entered the market to 32 percent two years later. Smoking rates among male Korean teenagers rose from 18 percent to 30 percent in one year after import restrictions were removed. Thailand, Vietnam, Cambodia and China have been more recent targets for the giant tobacco companies. In those nations an estimated 25-30 percent of all smokers are now under the age of 20 years.

In a sad twist of irony, the cigarette industry's most recent target has been Vietnam, where it is taking advantage of lax laws and virtually nonexistent advertising controls. An estimated two million Vietnamese died during the war as a result of U.S. involvement. Two decades after the last U.S. soldiers departed, the killing of Vietnamese at U.S. hands is beginning again, this time, curiously, with the passive complicity of investment-starved Vietnamese officials.

In Vietnam the tobacco companies, true to form, have begun to target the young with a multi-million-dollar advertising campaign that glorifies the use of tobacco products as a model for enviable Western lifestyles. Little shame or conscience here.

The World Health Organization sees overseas tobacco-related deaths soaring in the years ahead, to at least seven million annually by the year 2020. While some in the U.S. churches have been working diligently to bring these practices and dangers to public light, most church leaders have done little to scrutinize these

A TOBACCO VIRUS

Today, tobacco use has spread to all parts of the world and is a major drain on the world's financial resources. A World Bank economist has estimated the net loss as a result of tobacco use at $200 billion per year, with half of these losses occurring in developing countries. The driving force behind the spread of this epidemic is not a virus, or a gene, or a natural disaster. It is man-made and is driven by the search for profit. This search for profit gives higher priority to the financial well-being of a few corporations than to the lives of hundreds of millions of people.

"World Tobacco Cost," **Tobacco Alert** newsletter, American Association for World Health, 1995.

practices. Social, economic and moral issues are involved here and these need full public disclosure and attention.

EXPANDING GLOBAL INTERESTS

Thomas C. Parrish

Thomas C. Parrish is Vice President of Corporate Affairs for Monk-Austin, International, Inc. Monk-Austin, International, Inc. is an international leaf dealer which sources flue-cured and burley tobacco from fifteen tobacco producing countries and sells to tobacco product manufacturers around the world.

■ POINTS TO CONSIDER

1. Discuss the trends in tobacco production in the past two decades. What has been the result of expanded production coinciding with worldwide consumption trends?

2. List and explain the various reasons why American producers are at a competitive disadvantage in the world market.

3. Describe the economic impact of U.S. tobacco exports.

4. Why does Parrish believe that U.S. trade policy is discriminatory toward tobacco?

Excerpted from the testimony of Thomas C. Parrish before the Subcommittee on Specialty Crops and Natural Resources of the House of Representatives Agriculture Committee, June 11, 1994.

Expanding global market is where there are real opportunities for future long term growth.

Our future growth is tied directly to the increasing market for tobacco products in countries outside the United States. Therefore, we must focus our corporate attention on effectively supplying the needs of our customers here at home and abroad. During the past decade, we have watched other countries around the world expand their tobacco production while our output here in the United States has declined.

WORLDWIDE GROWTH

Since 1980, worldwide flue-cured production has grown by almost 120% – production is up 303% in China, 83% in Brazil, and 71% in Zimbabwe. Production is also up in India, the Philippines, Argentina and Italy. During those 13 years, U.S. output of flue-cured dropped 18.5% while our share of world production fell from 20% to 7.4%.

Since 1980, worldwide burley production has grown nearly 73% – production has expanded 521% in Malawi, nearly 335% in Brazil, and 240% in China. Production is also up in the Philippines, Argentina, Thailand and Mexico. During those 13 years, U.S. output of burley declined 13.3%. In 1980, 44% of the world's burley tobacco was produced in the United States. Last year, the U.S. share was 29%.

Clearly, the geography of tobacco production is shifting dramatically. Not only has the geography shifted, but since 1990, total world tobacco production has expanded 21% while consumption has grown only 12%. The result: annual production surpluses that have left us with excessive inventories of leaf tobacco worldwide.

Exports of U.S. leaf tobacco fell 20% last year, mainly as a result of the world oversupply. Excess inventories depressed prices and heightened worldwide competition in the world market. Most of the U.S. export decline comes from reduced sales to all of our traditional markets in Europe and Asia. If you compare 1994 U.S. exports to 1992 levels, you will find sales to Germany were down 44%; to Turkey, down 17%; to the Netherlands, down 24%; and to the United Kingdom, down 14%. Shrinking consumption is not the problem in all of these markets. The problem is that our traditional customers are looking elsewhere for tobacco. Why?

COMPETITIVE DISADVANTAGE

In general, U.S. tobacco producers are at a competitive disadvantage in the world market for three reasons: (1) Farm level prices in other producing countries are generally lower than in the United states – and are falling; (2) The quality of foreign leaf is improving; and (3) Quality itself is no longer as critical to cigarette blends as it was in the past.

Our traditional customers in Europe and Asia are battling national and regional economic recessions. As shrewd businessmen, they look for ways to keep their cost down. In addition to adjusting inventories, many also turn to lower priced leaf markets to meet their buying needs.

We can understand and sympathize with the frustration felt by U.S. tobacco growers at the dramatic increase in imports of foreign tobacco in recent years. However, it is an unfortunate fact that rising imports are a symptom of the problem and not the problem itself. U.S. tobacco is not immune to economic or market realities. The dramatic growth and consumption of generic cigarettes, not only in the United States but elsewhere in the world, has created strong pressures on manufacturers to lower cost inputs. U.S. tobacco remains the highest priced in the world, and is, therefore, at a significant disadvantage when it comes to satisfying this new demand for a lower priced cigarette.

Tom Capehart and Verner Grise articulated the challenge to American growers very well during their presentation to the Tobacco Marketing Cost Study Committee. They said: "The challenge to the American tobacco grower is clear. A number of nations are producing competitively priced quality leaf while the demand for very high quality leaf is decreasing. New markets for leaf and cigarettes will develop in the coming decades, for demand will be for cheap, low-quality tobacco. The coming decade will see greater emphasis on price. Unless U.S. farmers address the price issue, our share of world leaf trade will continue to shrink."

FUTURE DIRECTION

It appears to us that some leaders in the U.S. tobacco growing community are willing to tie their future to a declining domestic market. Any short term benefit gained from reducing imports will be offset in the long run by weakening our competitive position in

143

the world market. Although import restrictions may stabilize flue-cured and burley quotas for the next year or two, in the long run, they have set in motion what may prove to be irreversible losses on the export side. As an international merchant, we think that the expanding global market is where there are real opportunities for future long-term growth.

If you think our perspective is credible, let's examine the U.S. situation from the standpoint of a foreign purchaser of U.S. tobac-co. Many traditional purchasers of U.S. tobacco are still willing to pay a premium for U.S. tobacco. However, when they are asked to pay a price that is based on an artificial price support and which carries additional cost and adds no value to the product, they often balk. They ask us why they should pay for excessive quota lease rates, very high marketing cost, high assessments, and what they perceive to be unnecessary and unreasonable adminis-trative costs of compliance with government regulations when they can find acceptable substitutes elsewhere. We all – govern-ment, growers, warehousemen and dealers – need to work toward reducing the cost of U.S. leaf.

TOBACCO EXPORT IMPACT

The anti-smoking lobby is using the Department of Health and Human Services in an attempt to dictate U.S. export policy with respect to tobacco and tobacco products. This manner of setting trade policy is both unprecedented and misguided. Furthermore, in the context of trade, the health issue is irrelevant since many countries already grow tobacco and manufacture tobacco prod-ucts.

More importantly, the export of U.S. tobacco has an enormous positive economic impact on the U.S. tobacco industry and the U.S. economy. The following is a partial listing of numerous facts which well illustrate the direct contribution made by U.S. tobacco exports:

• In 1993, the United States exported leaf tobacco and tobacco products valued at $5.6 billion.

• U.S. tobacco trade contributed more than $4 billion to the nation's balance of trade in 1993.

• Exports of manufactured tobacco products in 1993 totaled $4.2 billion – 92.3% of which was earned by cigarette exports.

144

Tobacco products contributed $3.6 billion to the nation's trade balance in 1993.

• In 1992, tobacco net trade generated a surplus of $4.9 billion. By comparison, total U.S. net trade produced a deficit of $84.5 billion in 1992.

• In 1992, tobacco exports supported 299,255 jobs in the United States, generating approximately $7.1 billion in total compensation and $2.0 billion in tax revenue.

• The export of tobacco is one of the few U.S. industries that produces a trade surplus with the principal trade regions of East Asia, Europe and the Middle East.

These facts illustrate the magnitude of the impact that tobacco exports have on all facets of the U.S. economy ranging from local employment to reducing the U.S. trade deficit. The parties who will suffer from a curtailment of U.S. tobacco exports for health reasons will be American growers and exporters. Therefore, we strongly oppose any actions designed to restrict or ban tobacco exports.

PROHIBITION OF USING FEDERAL FUNDS TO PROMOTE TOBACCO EXPORTS

The Agricultural Appropriations bill passed recently prohibits the tobacco industry from using Market Promotion Program and Cooperator Foreign Market Development funds and prohibits the USDA from paying salaries of personnel promoting tobacco exports.

It is our position that the U.S. government should continue treating the U.S. tobacco export trade as a very important part of the total U.S. trading economy. Any effort to inhibit U.S. tobacco exports ostensibly to protect the health of citizens in other countries is misguided. Supplies of tobacco are readily available from many other countries that are successfully competing in the international market. These competing countries will quickly fill gaps resulting from a failure to promote the export of U.S. tobacco.

SINGLING OUT TOBACCO

The United States government should pursue a non-discriminatory export policy which gives equal emphasis to promoting exports of all legal U.S. commodities and manufactured goods. It seems the position of the federal government is that promoting tobacco exports is tantamount to promoting smoking. We contend this is not the case. There is a big difference between the two. Penalizing U.S. growers by eliminating tobacco export promotion programs will in no way affect the use of tobacco products in other countries. Elimination of export promotion programs for tobacco will do irreparable harm to American efforts to penetrate emerging markets in the former Soviet Bloc nations and elsewhere.

The importance of market openings in recent years should not be overlooked. U.S. growers and exporters have benefited by the opening of markets in Japan, Thailand, Taiwan and others. It is unfair and unwise to single out tobacco for exclusion from market promotion programs in view of the tremendous contribution the industry makes to our economy and government. Again, the parties who suffer by a change in the market opening policy will be American tobacco growers, manufacturers and exporters.

The challenge is clear: We must all have the courage to accept and implement significant change. We are committed to doing our part to assure a positive future for the U.S. tobacco trade.

READING

23

SMOKERS SAVE SOCIETY MONEY

W. Kip Viscusi

W. Kip Viscusi wrote this article when he was the George G. Allen Professor of Economics at Duke University. He now teaches at Harvard.

■ **POINTS TO CONSIDER**

1. List the various rationales for imposing a cigarette tax.

2. Discuss the various externalities (cost to others) of smoking.

3. What is the conclusion of the study?

4. Do smokers pay their way through current taxes imposed? Explain.

W. Kip Viscusi, "Cigarette Taxation and the Social Consequences of Smoking." Prepared for the 1994 National Bureau of Economic Research Conference on Tax Policy and the Economy, Washington, D.C., November 1, 1994.

The cost savings that result because of the premature deaths of smokers through their lower Social Security and pension costs will more than compensate for the added costs imposed by smokers, chiefly through higher health insurance costs.

Detailed calculations of the financial externalities (cost to society) of smoking indicate that the financial savings from premature mortality in terms of lower nursing home costs and retirement pensions exceed the higher medical care and life insurance costs generated. The costs of environmental tobacco smoke are highly uncertain, but of potentially substantial magnitude. Even with recognition of these costs, current cigarette taxes exceed the magnitude of the estimated net externalities.

INTRODUCTION

Cigarette smoking has long been the object of social controversy and policy interventions. However, in recent years this scrutiny has become greater...There are many reasons why, from a political standpoint, taxes might be imposed. One possible explanation is political expediency. Cigarette smokers now constitute a minority of the population. Moreover, given the social controversy pertaining to smoking, they are a vulnerable minority for which there will be lower political costs associated with taxation than, for example, with a more broadly based tax.

There may also be legitimate economic rationales for taxing cigarettes, wholly apart from the desire to raise revenues. Cigarette taxes and alcohol taxes are among the most widely used forms of "sin taxes." The economic rationale for such taxes is that imposing taxes discourages behavior that may be associated with inefficient decisions. The inadequacies in behavior may pertain to the choices by smokers with respect to their own well-being or that of their families. Taxes could be imposed to align these decisions with what would prevail if individual choices were rational from a self-interest standpoint. A second impetus for taxation would arise if there were net external costs imposed on the rest of society by cigarette smoking. In that case, cigarette taxes would function much like a tax to lead smokers to internalize the external costs of their actions...

148

SOCIAL COSTS

The externality aspects of smoking likewise involve competing effects. Cigarette smokers have no private incentive to internalize all of the effects of smoking on others, but these effects are not necessarily adverse on balance. To the extent that cigarette smoking leads to adverse health consequences, there will be higher health insurance costs associated with these illnesses as well as other social externalities, such as life insurance costs. However, there may also be offsetting costs savings from earlier mortality through reduced costs of pensions, Social Security, Medicare, and health expenditures later in life. In tallying these externalities, one should also take into account any adverse health effects of environmental tobacco smoke to the extent that these can be reliably estimated. It is not clear *a priori* whether the cost savings to society are exceeded by the costs imposed on society. Resolving these issues requires a detailed empirical assessment of the competing influences...

A particularly controversial class of externalities linked to smoking consists of the insurance cost effects arising from the estimated health consequences of smoking. States such as Mississippi and Florida are initiating lawsuits in an attempt to recoup state Medicaid payments. Hillary Clinton and the Clinton Administration more generally have used the argument that cigarette smoking leads to higher health insurance costs as a rationale for a higher cigarette tax. There has also begun to develop a growing sense in the media that smokers are not paying their own way.

This perception contrasts with the results of economic studies of externalities. Assessments by Shoven, Sundberg, and Bunker (1989), Manning et al. (1989, 1991), and Gravelle and Zimmerman (1994) all suggest that consideration of the insurance-related externalities is more complex than many public observers have noted. In particular, if smoking indeed leads to premature death, then there will be competing influences. Higher health care costs may be imposed in the short run, but these deaths may save society additional resources later in life, since these smokers will not be able to collect Social Security and pension benefits for the same amount of time. Which effect is larger is an empirical issue. Moreover, when one is assessing these externalities, it is certainly not appropriate to tally only the potential adverse consequences of smoking, such as the effects on Medicaid or health insurance costs, and to neglect systematically the estimated cost savings to society. Proper assessment requires that all legitimate effects be considered.

The most comprehensive study to date is that by Manning et al. (1991), which also forms the basis for much of the analysis in Gravelle and Zimmerman (1994). The approach here will be to take the study by Manning et al. (1991) as the baseline and to update it in a variety of ways. These revisions will include much more than recognition of price changes through shifts in the consumer price index. Rather, using their study as a baseline, the estimates were completely reworked to reflect the changing cost of health insurance as well as our increased understanding of the role of smoking...

The main areas of cost savings are nursing home care and retirement pensions. Since smokers die sooner, they will spend less time in nursing homes, leading to a cost savings of $0.23 per pack. In addition, they will be collecting their pensions and Social Security benefits for a shorter period, leading to a costs savings of $1.19 per pack. Since smokers die sooner, society loses the taxes it could have reaped on their earnings. The health and Social Security tax losses from these effects average –$0.40 per pack. The total net costs of smokers to society are –$0.30 per pack. The fire costs reflect only the insurance costs, which adjusted Manning et al.'s (1991) estimates to account for current estimates of fire-related damage. Subsequently, fire-related mortality costs outside the home will be added as well, which is another new feature of this study...

In effect, smokers are already paying their own way in the sense that there is a net externality cost savings to society from their smoking because of the cost savings arising from their premature deaths. These figures exclude from consideration the cigarette taxes already paid by smokers. Thus, there is a net cost savings from the externalities as well as an additional infusion of tax revenues from smokers. Taken at face value, these estimates indicate that cigarette smoking should be subsidized rather than taxed.

CONCLUSION

Smokers now pay an average of $0.53 per pack in cigarette taxes. If our objective is to set an appropriate tax level to reflect the externalities generated by cigarettes, the question then becomes whether this tax is sufficient to address the externality costs imposed.

These costs consist of several potential elements. The first of these – the externalities to the smoker's future self – appear to be unimportant. Very few smokers underestimate the hazards associated with smoking, and indeed, overall, smokers over-assess the risks of smoking. To the extent that smokers also internalize the environmental tobacco smoke (ETS) risks to household members, this effect would be captured as well in these private decisions.

The focal point of the externality cost debate has not been losses to the smokers' future selves but on the health insurance and related costs associated with smoking. A comprehensive assessment of these costs suggests that on balance, smokers do not cost society resources because of their smoking activities, but rather save society money. Evidence indicates that at reasonable rates of discount, the cost savings that result because of the premature deaths of smokers through their lower Social Security and pension costs will more than compensate for the added costs imposed by smokers, chiefly through higher health insurance costs. Thus, not only is there not a rationale for imposing a tax due to these insurance-related externalities, but rather on balance there is a net cost savings to society even excluding consideration of the current cigarette taxes paid by smokers.

The principal externality cost component that might provide the impetus for a cigarette tax consists of ETS costs. Environmental tobacco smoke, however, is now the target of a wide range of explicit regulatory proposals that would limit public exposure to ETS. Legislation before Congress would ban smoking in public places. The Occupational Safety and Health Administration has proposed a regulation that would ban smoking in the workplace except in situations where a designated smoking area meeting stringent ventilation conditions was provided. If these measures are enacted, it would not be appropriate to consider the current levels of external cost of ETS in setting the appropriate tax level because the public externalities would have been addressed by an alternative policy tool, direct regulation.

READING

24

THE "COST" OF SMOKING IS TOO HIGH

Jeffrey E. Harris

Jeffrey E. Harris, M.D., Ph.D. is a practicing primary care internist at the Massachusetts General Hospital in Boston and an economics professor at the Massachusetts Institute of Technology.

■ POINTS TO CONSIDER

1. Summarize the economic cost to society of smoking according to Harris.

2. Describe the difference, according to the author, between "warm" and "cold" economics. What external or social costs does Harris calculate that many "cold" economists do not take into account?

3. Why does the author object to including in cost estimates of smoking, the amount saved in Social Security and retirement benefits?

4. Overall, summarize the various effects of a $.75 per-pack increase on cigarettes.

5. Why does Harris contend that cigarettes are a special case among consumer products that are detrimental to health?

Excerpted from the testimony of Jeffrey E. Harris before the House of Representatives Ways and Means Committee, November 18, 1993.

I have estimated the health care costs of smoking that are subsidized by persons who never smoked. These costs vastly understate the total burden of smoking imposed on our society.

Cigarette smoking is now responsible for twenty percent of all deaths in the United States annually. As a physician, I have personally witnessed the tragedy of disability and death wrought by smoking. While I shall address questions of economic cost, I emphasize that smoking is first and foremost a health issue. When we talk about disease in dollar terms, we should take care not to trivialize the human lives at stake.

From my review of past and ongoing research, I estimate that cigarette smoking accounts for 8 percent of all health care spending in the United States. The range of uncertainty in my estimate is from 4.2 percent to 11.5 percent.

COST OF SMOKING

By 1995, national health expenditures are projected to reach $1.1 trillion, or 15.5 percent of Gross Domestic Product (GDP). Accordingly, in 1995, by my estimate, the adverse health effects of cigarette smoking will be responsible for $88 billion in health care spending, with an uncertainty range of $46 to $127 billion.

Cigarette smokers represent 18 percent of the entire U.S. population (including infants and children). Former smokers make up another 19 percent of the population. Sixty-three percent of the population has never smoked. Accordingly, under universal health coverage, I estimate that in 1995, people who never smoked will contribute $55 billion toward the health care costs of cigarette smoking. (The uncertainty range is from $30 to $80 billion.) Current and former smokers will pay the remaining $33 billion. (The uncertainty range is $17 to $47 billion.)

With no intervening increase in federal cigarette taxes, I expect U.S. cigarette consumption in 1995 to be 23.7 billion packs. At that level of cigarette consumption, the health care financing burden imposed upon people who never smoked would amount to $2.32 per pack (with an uncertainty range from $1.27 to $3.38 per pack). The full health care costs of smoking, including those costs borne by current and former smokers, would amount to $3.71 per pack (with an uncertainty range from $1.94 to $5.36 per pack).

EXTERNAL COSTS: WARM ECONOMICS VERSUS COLD ECONOMICS

I have estimated the health care costs of smoking that are subsidized by persons who never smoked. These costs vastly understate the total burden of smoking imposed on our society. Many of these "external" or "social" costs are easy to describe but difficult to quantify. Some economists focus only on the easy-to-measure costs; they assume that all unquantifiable costs somehow cancel each other out. I call this the "cold approach." As a physician, I know that the cold, hard numbers don't tell the whole story, that one cannot dismiss injury and suffering merely because it cannot be simply calibrated. I prefer the alternative "warm approach."

The death and disease caused by smoking results in a loss of American productivity. According to the Centers for Disease Control, in 1990, the death toll from smoking caused an annual loss of 1.1 million person-years of life before the age of 65. This loss of productivity has numerous macro-economic consequences – for example, reduced international competitiveness – that are real, but difficult to quantify.

In a May 1993 report, the Office of Technology Assessment (OTA) estimated that premature deaths from smoking (along with lost work-days and productivity) caused a loss of $47.2 billion in personal income tax in 1990. At current inflation rates, that amounts to $56 billion in 1995. At a 25 percent marginal tax rate, OTA's estimated productivity loss would mean foregone income taxes of $14 billion, which might otherwise help to pay for national defense, environmental protection, drug enforcement, crime control, and other needed federal services. As a "warm" economist, I cannot brush aside these hard-to-quantify external costs.

COLD ECONOMICS

"Cold" economists assume that smokers and their families privately, rationally, and voluntarily bear the costs from smoking-related disease and death. This is a fiction that ignores the dual reality of teenage initiation into cigarettes and adult addiction to cigarettes.

The average American smoker now starts regular cigarette use at age fifteen, and many Americans start before age ten. Teens and pre-teens typically believe that they can stop at will. Yet each year, at least 17 million adult smokers try to quit but fail. On any single attempt to quit, the smoker's long-term success rate may be as low as 8 percent. Adult cigarette smokers have cumulatively paid billions of dollars for all sorts of over-the-counter and prescription smoking cessation aids, and most market analysts believe that the pent-up demand for such products is enormous. A "warm" economist recognizes that current cigarette smokers would collectively be willing to pay billions of dollars to have their addiction taken away from them. This external cost is hard to quantify, but again, it is genuine.

"Cold" economists say that a person who dies upon retirement saves the federal purse and private pension plans the costs of Social Security benefits and retirement annuities. "Warm" economists say that this is not the kind of calculation that a civilized society engages in. According to the "cold" approach, society incurs additional external costs for each and every extra day that they survive and serve our country.

When Congress considers the merits of increasing federal funding for breast cancer prevention, diagnosis and treatment, it does not remind itself that most women who die from breast cancer have already passed their sixty-fifth birthdays. It does not consider whether an improvement in breast cancer survival would impose a burden on Social Security or private pensions. Congress considers the funding of breast cancer research primarily a matter of health. The same standard should apply to the taxation of cigarettes.

Senator Moynihan has proposed a tax on ammunition to help finance the Administration's Health Security Act. When Congress considers this proposal, I hope that it does not consider the age distribution of the victims of fatal shootings, or the savings in external costs that might accrue if septuagenarians were murdered. We should apply the same standard when we consider measures to reduce the death toll from smoking. No double standard for cigarette smoking should be applied.

During the fiscal year ending June 30, 1993, total governmental taxes on cigarettes – including federal, state and local excise taxes as well as applicable state sales taxes – amounted to $0.58 per pack. Of this amount $0.24 per pack represented the current federal excise tax. Accordingly, even with an additional federal tax of $0.75 per pack, I believe that the total tax burden on cigarettes would fall far short of its true social cost.

155

IMPACTS OF CIGARETTE TAXATION

If that tax ($.75) per pack were fully reflected in the retail price of cigarettes, then I estimate that U.S. cigarette consumption would decline about 12 percent. Most of the resulting drop in smoking rates would represent adults quitting smoking and teenagers never starting. Altogether, there could be as many as four million fewer cigarette smokers. The adult quitters will experience immediate health benefits in terms of reduced rates of cardiovascular disease, and more long-term benefits in terms of reduced rates of cancer and chronic lung disease. The teenagers who never started will add years to their life expectancy.

Some have argued that an increase in the federal excise tax will cost the U.S. economy millions of jobs. These claims are markedly exaggerated. For a full discussion, I refer to a recent report by Arthur Andersen Economic Consulting. The primary, direct negative impact an increase in the federal excise tax will be on American cigarette manufacturers and their shareholders – not retailers or farmers. The adverse impact on cigarette manufacturers will be greater if the $.75 tax is not fully passed on to consumers.

Cigarette manufacturers have known for months that the federal tax on cigarettes would rise from its current level of $.24 per pack to nearly $1.00 per pack. Temporary price reductions, announced recently by Philip Morris and other companies, were intended partly to alleviate the impact of higher future taxes. During the first part of 1993, manufacturers' wholesale prices for king-size cigarettes were cut by $.37 per pack. The increasing market shares of discount and generic cigarettes will also blunt the price effect of a federal tax increase.

The Treasury Department estimates that a $.75 per-pack tax would net $11 billion in additional federal dollars in the first year alone. If the $.75 tax increase were fully passed on to consumers, then I estimate the first-year impact to be closer to $12 billion. Still, the Treasury's estimate is within the margin of uncertainty of my own calculations.

CONCLUSION

Some may ask: if we tax cigarettes because they are detrimental to health, then why don't we also tax the saturated fat in tenderloin beef cuts, or extra salt in salted peanuts? But tobacco products are a unique and special case. They cause serious harm when used exactly as intended. What is more, cigarettes are toxic to all smokers at every dose.

By contrast, beef contains important nutrients including protein and essential amino acids. Peanuts contain Vitamin E, for one, and as some researchers note, eating nuts may help prevent heart disease. For many people, eating saturated fats does not raise blood cholesterol. For others, eating salt does not cause hypertension. In short, I do not see the taxation of tobacco for health reasons as pushing our society down an inevitably slippery slope.

I have estimated that in 1995, under universal health insurance, people who never smoked will pay $55 billion toward the health care costs of smoking. This is one of many important, but less quantifiable external costs of cigarette use. The $11 to $12 billion increase in net revenues in 1995 – to be derived from the Administration's proposed cigarette tax hike – will not come close to covering these external costs.

Still, I must again emphasize as a physician that smoking is foremost a health problem, not a matter of cold economic calculation. Health care reform is about saving lives. When I tell one patient that she has inoperable lung cancer, when I urge another to quit before he has a fatal heart attack, I don't ask myself whether their illnesses are raising or lowering the federal deficit. I just think about getting them better.

RECOGNIZING AUTHOR'S POINT OF VIEW

This activity may be used as an individualized study guide for students in libraries and resource centers or as a discussion catalyst in small group and classroom discussions.

Many readers are unaware that written material usually expresses an opinion or bias. The capacity to recognize an author's point of view is an essential reading skill. The skill to read with insight and understanding involves the ability to detect different kinds of opinions or bias. **Sex bias, race bias, ethnocentric bias, political bias** and **religious bias** are five basic kinds of opinions expressed in editorials and all literature that attempts to persuade. They are briefly defined in the glossary below.

Five Kinds of Editorial Opinion or Bias

Sex Bias – the expression of dislike for and/or feeling of superiority over the opposite sex or a particular sexual minority

Race Bias – the expression of dislike for and/or feeling of superiority over a racial group

Ethnocentric Bias – the expression of a belief that one's own group, race, religion, culture or nation is superior. Ethnocentric persons judge others by their own standards and values.

Political Bias – the expression of political opinions and attitudes about domestic or foreign affairs

Religious Bias – the expression of a religious belief or attitude

Guidelines

1. Locate three examples of **political opinion** or **bias** in the readings from Chapter Five.

2. Locate five sentences that provide examples of any kind of **editorial opinion** or **bias** from the readings in Chapter Five.

3. Write down the above sentences and determine what kind of bias each sentence represents. Is it **sex bias, race bias, ethnocentric bias, political bias** or **religious bias?**

4. Make up one-sentence statements that would be an example of each of the following: **sex bias, race bias, ethnocentric bias, political bias** and **religious bias.**

5. See if you can locate five sentences that are **factual** statements from the readings in Chapter Five.

Summarize author's point of view in one sentence for each of the following opinions:

Reading 18 _____

Reading 19 _____

Reading 20 _____

Reading 21 _____

Reading 22 _____

Reading 23 _____

Reading 24 _____

6. Read through the source descriptions on the next page. Choose one of the source descriptions that best describes each reading in Chapter Five.

Source Descriptions

a. Essentially an article that relates factual information

b. Essentially an article that expresses editorial points of view

c. Both of the above

d. None of the above

After careful consideration, pick out one source that you agree with the most.

INDEX

BIBLIOGRAPHY

Magazine References

Alonzo, Vincent. "Up in Smoke." **Incentive**, June 1996: 43-46.

Bates, Eric. "Tobacco Industry Uses Influence to Intimidate." **Mother Jones**, March 1996: 27.

"Bill Clinton vs. Joe Camel." **U.S. News & World Report**, Sept. 2, 1996: 12.

Buton, Graham. "The Great Performer." **Forbes, Law and Issues**, Oct. 21, 1996: 74.

Carey, John. "Clinton's Antismoking Plan Won't Exactly Kick Butt." **Business Week**, Sept. 9, 1996: 42.

Chapman, Simon. "Tobacco Control." **British Medical Journal**, July 13, 1996: 97.

Cohen, Jon. "Tobacco Money Lights Up a Debate." **Science**, April 26, 1996: 488.

Colwell, Brian. "The Giant Texas Smoke Scream" **Journal of School Health**, Aug. 1996: 210.

Curley, Bob. "Clinton Wields Big Stick Against Big Tobacco." **Alcoholism & Drug Abuse Week**, Sept. 2, 1996: 5.

"Democratic Buttheads." **The Weekly Standard**, July 22, 1996: 3.

DeMont, John. "Tobacco's Top Guns." **Maclean's**, Nov. 18, 1996: 18.

Dentzer, Susan. "Can Farmers Kick the Habit, Too?" **U.S. News & World Report**, Oct. 7, 1996: 56.

Driedger, Sharon Doyle. "Toronto Butts Out." **Maclean's**, Canada, July 15, 1996: 16.

"Epidemiology Versus a Smoke Screen." **Lancet**, Aug. 10, 1996: 410.

France, Mike. "Who Got Smoked in Indianapolis?" **Business Week**, Sept. 9, 1996: 44.

163

France, Mike. "The World War on Tobacco." **Business Week,** Nov. 11, 1996: 99.

Gladwell, Malcolm. "Freedom's Smoke." **The New Republic,** Nov. 4, 1996: 27.

Greenwald, John. "Cereal Showdown; By Slashing Prices 20%, the Post Division of Philip Morris Hopes to Regain Business." **Time,** April 29, 1996: 60.

Greising, David. "The Race Around the FDA." **Business Week,** Sept. 9, 1996: 38.

Guiltinan, Joseph P. and Gregory T. Gundlach. "Aggressive and Predatory Pricing: A Framework for Analysis." **Journal of Marketing,** Summer 1996: 87.

Gurrin, L Burton. "Effects of Maternal Smoking During Pregnancy." **Lancet,** Oct. 19, 1996: 1060.

Hernandez, Debra Gersh. "Tobacco Ad Debate Rages." **Editor & Publisher Magazine,** Sept. 7, 1996: 24.

Hess, John L. "Ashes to Ashes: America's Hundred-Year Cigarette War." **The Nation,** May 13, 1996: 28.

Hess, John L. "The Cigarette Papers." **The Nation,** May 13, 1996: 28.

Horton, Richard. "Playing With Smoke, But Not Without Fire." **The Lancet,** June 29, 1996: 1782.

"Ifs and Butts." **The Economist,** U.S. Edition, Aug. 31, 1996: 25.

Lacayo, Richard. "Put Out the Butt, Junior." **Time,** Sept. 2, 1996: 51.

Lefton, Terry and Mark Adams. "Philip Morris Plans Magazine." **Mediaweek,** Jan. 8, 1996: 4.

Mintz, Morton. "Keep States from Raising Cigarette Taxes." **Washington Monthly,** May 1996: 20.

Moore, Amity K. "Screening Smokes." **Supermarket News,** Sept. 16, 1996: 39.

Mundy, Alicia. "Magazine Pages Will Burn." **Mediaweek,** Oct. 14, 1996: 22-24.

Mundy, Alicia. "Philip Morris Has the Media Right Where It Wants It." **Mediaweek**, May 27, 1996: 22.

Neff, David. "Butt Out: It's High Time We Saved Children from the Tobacco Industry." **Christianity Today**, Oct. 28, 1996: 12.

Noland, Melody Powers. "Tobacco Prevention in Tobacco Raising Areas." **Journal of School Health**, Sept. 1996: 266.

O'Sullivan, Tom. "Kicking Butt." **Marketing Week**, Sept. 6, 1996: 41-43.

Pooley, Eric. "Peering Through the Smoke." **Time**, July 15, 1996: 20.

"Recall of Philip Morris Cigarettes." **Morbidity and Mortality Weekly Report**, March 29, 1996: 251.

Reid, Donald. "Teenage Drug Use: On the Increase, and Clear Links with Advertising and Sports Sponsorship." **British Medical Journal**, Aug. 17, 1996: 375.

Shaw, Russell. "Say Good-bye to Tobacco." **Mediaweek**, Sept. 9, 1996: MQ33.

Shepherd, Catherine. "Burning Up in Asia: More Smoking Means a Sharp Rise in Disease." **Asiaweek**, July 5, 1996: 55.

Stone, Peter H. "Blue Smoke and Mirrors." **The National Journal**, May 4, 1996: 1016.

Sugarman, Stephen D. "Ashes to Ashes: America's Hundred-Year Cigarette War." **Science**, Aug. 9, 1996: 744.

Sugarman, Stephen D. "The Cigarette Papers." **Science**, Aug. 9, 1996: 744.

Sugarman, Stephen D. "Smokescreen: The Truth Behind the Tobacco Industry Cover-Up." **Science**, Aug. 9, 1996: 744.

Sullum, Jacob. "Smoking Wars." **National Review**, July 29, 1996: 39.

Tang, Terry. "Big Tobacco's Denial Strategy Starting to Fail." **The Montgomery Advertiser**, June 13, 1996.

"Tobacco: Fuming on the Farm." **The Economist**, Oct. 12, 1996: 30.

"Tobacco: It's a Law-and-Order Issue." **Business Week**, Sept. 9, 1996: 132.

"Tobacco Use and High School Students." **Journal of School Health**, Aug. 1996: 222.

"Weed Whackers; Presidential Candidates Bill Clinton and Bob Dole." **Reason**, Nov. 1996: 8.

Zegart, Dan. "Buried Evidence: The Damaging Secret Documents and Testimony Tobacco Companies Tried to Suppress." **The Nation**, March 4, 1996: 11.

Book References

Allison, Patricia and Jack Yost. **Hooked – But Not Hopeless: Kicking Nicotine Addiction**, 1996, BridgeCity Bks.

Chandler, William U. **Banishing Tobacco**, 1986, Worldwatch Inst.

Dye, Christina. **Everyday Drugs & Pregnancy: Alcohol, Tobacco & Caffeine**, rev. ed., 1994, Do It Now.

Elders, M. Jocelyn. **Preventing Tobacco Use Among Young People: A Report of the Surgeon General**, 1994, DIANE Pub.

Feighery, Ellen, et al. **Tobacco Free Youth: How To Reduce Sales to Minors in Your Community**, 1992, Stanford CRDP.

Gilbert, David G. **Smoking: Individual Differences, Psychopathology & Emotion**, 1995, Taylor & Francis.

Glantz, Stanton A., et al. **The Cigarette Papers**, 1996, U CA Pr.

Gold, Mark S. **Tobacco**, 1995, Plenum.

Harrington, John P. **Tobacco Among the Karuk Indians of California**, 1995, Rprt Serv.

Health Benefits of Smoking Cessation, 1995, Gordon Pr.

Health Benefits of Smoking Cessation: A Report of the Surgeon General, 1995, DIANE Pub.

The Health Consequences of Smoking: Cancer & Chronic Lung Disease in the Workplace: A Report of the Surgeon General, 1995, DIANE Pub.

Health Consequences of Smoking: Cardiovascular Disease: A Report of the Surgeon General (1983), 1995, DIANE pub.

Health Consequences of Smoking for Women: A Report of the Surgeon General, 1995, DIANE Pub.

Health Consequences of Smoking: Nicotine Addiction: A Report of the Surgeon General (1988), 1995, DIANE Pub.

Hilts, Philip J. Smokescreen: The Truth Behind the Tobacco Industry Cover-Up, Addison-Wesley.

It Can Be Done: A Smoke-Free Europe: Report of the First European Conference on Tobacco Policy, 1990, World Health.

Kasuga, H., ed. Environmental Tobacco Smoke, 1993, Spr-Verlag.

Lee, P. N. Environmental Tobacco Smoke & Mortality: A Detailed Review of Epidemiological Evidence Relating Environmental Tobacco Smoke to the Risk of Cancer, Heart Disease & Other Causes of Death in Adults Who Have Never Smoked, 1992, S Karger.

Mecklenburg, R.E., et al. Tobacco Effects in the Mouth, 1995, DIANE Pub.

Murtaugh, Paul A. Tobacco Scare Found Faked: Revealing the Biggest Science Scandal in History, 1992, Am Rights Coun.

Prevention Material for Intervention in Drug, Alcohol & Tobacco Abuse: Resource Guide, 1995, Gordon Pr.

Reducing the Health Consequences of Smoking: 25 Years of Progress: A Report of the Surgeon General, 1995, DIANE Pub.

Roemer, R. Legislative Action to Combat the World Tobacco Epidemic, 1993, World Health.

Rogozinski, J. Smokeless Tobacco in the Western World, 1990, Devin.

Zieve, Allison M., et al. Comments of Public Citizen, Inc. Regarding the FDA's Proposal to Regulate the Sale & Promotion of Tobacco to Minors, 1996, Pub Citizen Inc.